THE CUSTOMER IS KING!

THE CUSTOMER IS KING!

R. Lee Harris

ASQC Quality Press
Milwaukee, Wisconsin

THE CUSTOMER IS KING!

R. Lee Harris

Library of Congress Cataloging-in-Publication Data

Harris, R. Lee,
    The customer is king!/R. Lee Harris.
        p.   cm.
    Includes index.
    ISBN 0-87389-122-8
    1. Customer service.   I. Title.
    HF5415.5.H293 1991
    658.8'12—dc20   91-20527
                                                     CIP

1098765432

ISBN 0-87389-122-8

Acquisitions Editor: Jeanine L. Lau
Production Editor: Mary Beth Nilles
Set in 12-point Times by Patricia L. Coogan.
Cover design by Wayne Dober.
Printed and bound by BookCrafters.

For a free copy of the ASQC Quality Press Publications Catalog,
including ASQC membership information, call 800-952-6587.

Printed in the United States of America

ASQC Quality Press
611 East Wisconsin Avenue
Milwaukee, Wisconsin 53202

Printed on Recycled Paper

Dedicated to Dad and Mom who taught me the first rule of customer service…"do unto others as you would have them do unto you."

Contents

Preface

Picture this...you walk into a local department store. The sales-clerks are chatting with each other and don't bother to look your way. You finally pick out your purchase and head to the cashier. She is talking on the phone. You are left standing there without being acknowledged. Finally she rings your purchase and without looking at you says, "That'll be $37.50." You pay and nothing more is said to you as you leave. Now here's a sobering thought. Could this be your store? Could these be your employees?

This book is about customer service. A common sense approach to customer service. No complicated management strategies or psychological theories. Just plain, simple, basic horse sense.

I'm in the commercial real estate business, and my firm is pretty forward thinking when it comes to the belief that the customer is king. While some of the concepts explored in this book evolve from the real estate industry, its contents relate universally to all types of large and small companies. This book is written for anyone who deals directly with customers or who manages people with direct customer interaction. It will be of interest to sales-clerks, department managers, customer service representatives, chief executive officers, and others. It offers exciting and practical ideas that can serve as cornerstones toward building a program that enhances customer service.

CHAPTER 1

Customer Service Is An Attitude

C ustomer service has become society's buzzword; however, lip service is not enough! One must develop a customer service attitude. Once the belief that customers come first is established in mind and feeling, then the idea comes alive. The people involved will begin to eat, sleep, and breathe the concept. Creative ideas will begin to flow and new enthusiasm will spread throughout the organization.

A customer service attitude must begin at the very top of a company's organizational chart. The chairman of the board and the president/chief executive officer (CEO) must get actively involved. It is difficult to get employees on other levels to successfully render top-notch customer service when top management does not provide such a focus. If you are a CEO or rank high in your organization, bare your soul and ask yourself, "Do I truly have a customer service attitude?" Be honest and self-critical. There is no question that we can all do better. Test your level of sensitivity by answering the following questions:

- When was the last time I talked to a customer? Did I really listen to what that customer had to say?

- How often do I talk (and *really* listen) to my customers?

- What comes first—customer service or my profits?

- When is the last time I had a new idea to improve customer service? How often do I have such ideas?

- Do I make customer service a centerpiece of every staff meeting?

- Do I stop and think about how every decision I make impacts the level of customer service I provide?

- What is my first (gut) reaction to a customer's complaint or an irate customer?

Stay In Touch With The Customer

Constantly rubbing shoulders with your customers is one of the best ways to develop *and* maintain a customer service attitude. After all, what can be more true than the worn-out adage that it is the customers who keep food on all of our tables? Without continual contact with our customers, how can we truly be tuned in to their needs? There is a perception that CEOs of large corporations are insulated from reality by layers of bureaucracy, important meetings, financial reports, and the like. This un-doubtedly is correct in some cases. Smart CEOs, however, make it a priority to get in the trenches and make personal contact with their customers. Executives of the McDonald's restaurant chain spend time periodically working in their restaurants, not only to gain insight into day-to-day operations, but also to develop more customer awareness. It is reported that the legendary Sam Walton, founder of Wal-Mart, was visiting one of his stores in a small community when the computerized cash register system broke down. Walton grabbed a pad and pencil and began making note of the merchandise being purchased by those in the checkout line. A clerk then tallied the purchases on a calculator. Walton's actions were a reflection of his customer service philosophy. It was only natural for him to pitch in and do what he could to minimize the inconvenience of the moment. Undoubtedly this approach helped to make him a billionaire. Are you enough in touch with your customers to intuitively react to a similar situation?

Happy Customers = Profits

Does your bottom line (i.e., those quarterly earnings reports) take priority over customer service? Obviously a company has to watch expenses and strive to be as profitable as possible. At the same time, customer service does not have to cost a lot. As you will see later in this book, many ideas and techniques can be implemented at little or no cost.

If you dedicate your energies to seeing that your customers get the best possible products or services for their money, and see that these are delivered in an almost joyful manner, customer service will soon become your first priority. And guess what? Eventually you will profit beyond your wildest dreams. If this sounds like some sort of evangelical crusade, well, maybe it is. But there are countless examples of businesspeople who practice the concept of "what goes around comes around." They go above and beyond the call of duty to see that every need of their customers is met. In return they get customer loyalty, repeat business, referrals, and in some cases, the ability to charge a premium for superior products and services.

Fresh Ideas

Are you brimming over with new ideas on how to better serve your customers? Do you have a continuous stream of such ideas? Do you wake up in the middle of the night with a new thought on this subject? When you have a customer service attitude you will be able to answer these questions affirmatively.

Keep a customer service notebook handy. Ideas will begin to flow freely and you should write them all down. You should even go so far as to keep your notebook on your bedside table for those late-night inspirations. Set a goal to think of one new customer service concept each day. Don't worry about how major or minor it is, or how off the wall it may seem. Who knows, with some tinkering a few of the ideas might even become very productive, and you can always discard the true lemons.

Customer Service At The Staff Meeting

Is customer service a focus in your staff meetings? If the meeting leader doesn't take a moment to relate discussions to the firm's customer service efforts, then it is safe to say that no one else will either. If you are a meeting leader, suggest that everyone ponder the impact your decisions will have on your customers. If you aren't leading the meeting and this exercise is overlooked, speak up and suggest that it be done. A surefire way to see that this happens is to prepare an agenda where one of the items listed is, "What is the bottom line for our customers, as a result of our actions in this meeting?"

Irate Customers Can = Profits

How do you react when you get a complaint from a customer? Sometimes a customer can get pretty hostile and irate. Do you feel anger—outwardly or inwardly? Does your ego say "How dare this person tell me I have failed?" These are natural human emotions, but they aren't necessarily productive. Work toward seeing customer complaints as an *opportunity* to make a new friend and to turn "lemons into lemonade."

To some people, this idea is as comfortable as an old shoe. One of the owners of a midwestern funeral home received a call from a woman who didn't see her floral display at a service she attended. She was very upset and made quite a production out of the fact that she had paid $74 for the flowers. When the owner looked into the situation, he found that the display had mistakenly been used in another funeral that same day. Without any reservations, he called the woman and told her the truth about what had happened —then he wrote her a check for $74. People who have a customer service attitude will ignore the emotional distress that may be vented toward them and diplomatically resolve the customer's concern without becoming personally offended.

Customer Sensitivity Comes Naturally

It's easy to spot people whose mission to help other people is ingrained in their persona. Once I walked into a Payless Cashways building materials store and was looking at various hardware items. The salesclerk, an older gentleman, noticed I was eyeing an inexpensive power drill and offered some helpful hints toward selecting the right drill. He then helped me find the proper drill bits and walked halfway across the store to assist me in getting the correct-sized screw anchors—costing all of $0.06 apiece. This gentleman was memorable to me because he was genuinely interested in seeing that I made the right purchase to meet my needs—and he didn't seem to care if I spent $5, $50 or $500.

Walk into any Dillard's or Nordstrom's department store. These stores are staffed with friendly salespeople who continually offer their assistance. I have never been in a Dillard's store without being approached at least four times (and usually more often) by someone wanting to make sure I find what I am looking for. Even during the busy Christmas season this dedication to service is unwavering. If a salesperson is waiting on someone else, I am always acknowledged immediately. Sure, these two chains have excellent customer service training programs, but they also hire people who are already outgoing and have a caring attitude. Contrast this with the apathy and surliness that is displayed in many other large department stores. It's no wonder that Dillard's and Nordstrom's are perennially successful.

A Corporate Asset

Customer satisfaction can't be directly quantified on a corporate balance sheet, but it is definitely one of the most significant corporate assets a firm can possess. Roberto C. Goizueta, chairman, Board of Directors, and chief executive officer of The Coca-Cola Company says:

Consumer satisfaction...that's The Coca-Cola Company's most valuable asset...and the most valuable asset of any successful company. As a matter of fact, for any truly successful company, 'satisfaction' should really be an understatement of what consumers feel about its products. Through the nuts and bolts of quality assurance...through the power of its advertising... through its dedication to service...the truly successful company creates something beyond simple satisfaction. It creates an emotional bond between its products and its consumers.

Material used with permission of The Coca–Cola Company

Companies all over the nation are beginning to realize the importance of rediscovering the customer-comes-first philosophy. Complacency is beginning to give way to new methods of providing old-fashioned service with a smile. W.W. Grainger, Inc., a distributor of heating, air conditioning, electrical, and plumbing parts and equipment, saw its earnings decline in 1982 by 11% on lethargic sales. The firm realized that it was no longer "customer-friendly" and, in fact, had made it increasingly more difficult for customers to make purchases. Armed with fresh market research, Grainger retooled its operation to be more customer attentive, and annual financial results now indicate that the strategy is working.

At Delta Air Lines, Hollis L. Harris, former president and chief operating officer, called it "recapturing a singleness of purpose." He said, "Recapturing a singleness of purpose is a challenge of formidable proportions. Where does a company, an industry, or a country begin to recapture a singleness of purpose? In a system that salutes the law of supply and demand, the answer is simple enough and easily overlooked. The answer is one word and that word is: 'Customer'." Clearly the marketplace will recognize and reward those firms that put the customer first in terms of quality products that meet customers' needs; quality products that are fairly priced; and quality service that supports the products that are sold. As the world economy grows smaller through international trade, a wider selection of products and services will be offered to consumers. A company will either jump on the "Singleness of Purpose" bandwagon, or it will fail, as other companies will be standing in line to supplant it.

Everyday Actions

A customer service attitude is more than just a grand plan of monumental changes within an organization. It involves a lot of little everyday actions. A few examples:

- Returning all telephone calls the same day they are received.
- Answering all correspondence as quickly as possible.
- Sending personalized birthday cards to clients and/or customers.
- Calling a customer and explaining an invoice before it is sent.
- Clipping newspaper articles looking for information on clients and/or customers.
- Recalling customer preferences the next time they make a purchase.
- Offering a simple smile and friendly greeting to every customer within earshot.
- Cleaning up the mess repairpeople make while working in a customer's home or place of business.
- Taking the time by salespeople to learn all that they can about their products.
- Preparing understandable, easy, step-by-step instructions for assembling or using products.
- Having the same positive attitude at the end of the day as at the beginning.

Webster's defines a customer as "one who buys goods or services on a regular basis." To ensure that your company has "customers" in the true sense of the word, and not just one-time purchasers, the perspective of service must clearly come into focus for everyone in the organization. Says John F. Welch, Jr., chief executive officer of General Electric: "Serving the customer is, in the end, why we are here. Our general managers need to think of customer service as an investment—a win—not as an expense or nuisance. Sometimes people think they've risen too high in an organization to spend time on customer service. Leadership means, among other things, being passionate about customers…making heroes out of those who deal with customers every day."

A customer service attitude doesn't happen overnight. Roll the clock back and look at how you have operated in the past. Try and identify customer situations that you might not have handled quite as well as you would have liked. Write them down and laugh about them. Then decide how you will do things differently in the future. Challenge yourself to be open to new ideas that will create new approaches to enhance your customer sensitivity. Clip articles on the subject. Highlight the strong points and circulate them to your associates. Make a sign and tape it to the mirror in your bathroom reminding you of your new mission (maybe it could say, "The Customer Is King!"). The best way to gain a customer service attitude is to look for every way possible to affirm it in your consciousness. Sounds corny doesn't it? So what! A little corniness may be infectious and others may soon jump on the bandwagon, especially if they see how much fun you are having.

Action Plan

1. Customer service must begin at the very top of the organization with the chairman, president, and upper-level management.

2. Constantly rub shoulders with your customers to find out what they think. Keep from becoming insulated from reality by dwelling in an ivory tower.

3. As you interact with your customers, make sure you really listen. Don't hear what you want to hear. Listen to what they are saying.

4. Look for ways to crown the customer as king. Put the customer first, at the same time practicing sound business principles, and you won't have to worry about profits.

5. Keep the creative ideas flowing. Eat, breathe, and sleep customer service. New ideas will come to you as to how to demonstrate the customer attitude.

6. Make customer service the centerpiece of every staff meeting. It is critically important to reinforce the concept throughout the organization as often as possible.

7. As decisions are made, make certain that their impact on customers is always considered.

8. Look upon customer complaints (no matter how forceful they may be) as opportunities to make "lemonade out of lemons."

9. Hire employees who are intuitively service minded.

10. View customer service as your most important corporate asset and treat it as carefully as you would any other tangible investment.

11. Remember that if your company doesn't capture a single-ness of purpose, i.e., serving the customer, one of your competitors will do so.

12. Implement everyday little actions that will reflect the customer service attitude as well as making monumental, grand-plan changes.

CHAPTER 2

How Well Do You Know Your Customer?

T he late Walt Disney, referring to his empire, once said, "You don't build it for yourself. You know what the people want and you build it for them." The first step in a successful and ongoing customer service program is to know everything there is to know about your customers. Most people you ask will probably tell you they know their customers. On reflection, however, if they are honest with themselves, they will likely change their minds. It may even shock them to realize how little they really know about their customers. Some people have known their customers—20 years ago, or maybe even one year ago. But times are changing so quickly that understanding customers is a day-to-day effort. Businesspeople who aren't constantly in touch with their customers are unlikely to be in tune with their needs. And, if you don't truly know what your customers need, how can you provide the products or services that will meet those needs (and keep food on your table)?

Take an introspective look at yourself and your organization. Are you stuck in a rut? Have you gotten so busy and wrapped up in your daily routine that you may be taking your customers for granted? If you were really on top of things and knew your customers yesterday, do you know them today? How about tomorrow? Wipe the slate clean and resolve that from now on you will make the effort to understand your customers' needs on a daily basis. With a lifetime subscription to this philosophy, you are now ready to move ahead and take the next step.

Step One—Be A Good Listener

To understand your customers you must be a very good listener. Be prepared to listen to your customers, your employees, your suppliers, and everybody else in the loop of providing and receiving your products or services. Sometimes you may hear things that you don't want to hear. Listen anyway. Above all, do not try to impose your own beliefs and preferences on your customers. My company operates a number of apartment communities, and a recent fad has been the installation of ceiling fan/light fixture combinations. While these items may not have appeal to some of us, apartment residents have been highly enthusiastic about them. They don't cost very much. Often we must ignore our personal ideas and give the customers what they want. The bottom line—unless there are moral or ethical issues involved, don't make the mistake of trying to tell your customers what they want. Let them tell you.

American Express has a program whereby management personnel must devote two full days every quarter to making sales calls. This exercise serves several purposes including keeping managers from getting too entrenched in the "executive-itis" syndrome and reminding them to listen to customers. Arm and Hammer found that by listening to its customers it was able to discover new uses for its baking soda product such as deodorizing refrigerators and cleaning teeth. Being a good listener enabled Coca-Cola to start a bottler education project on proper storage and rotation techniques for products sweetened with aspartame, thus eliminating bitter diet soft drinks.

Step Two—Get Down In The Trenches

The best way to listen to your customers is through one-on-one personal encounters. Take a walk through your store, stop and have a chat with a customer. Call customers on the telephone or make appointments in their home and ask them questions about your products or services. People can be pretty candid when they are on their own turf. Don't do this once or twice, but try and rub shoulders with as many customers as time will permit every day.

As a result of getting down in the trenches, Kinder-Care Learning Centers, Inc., has been able to develop programs that address the needs and concerns of American families. Projects include Family Awareness; Muscular Dystrophy Association fundraising; Big Hearts, Little Hearts, an intergenerational program; and "Listen to Dolly," a child abuse awareness program. Kinder-Care has also created Bucklebear, emphasizing seatbelt safety.

Consider implementing a program in which all managerial personnel must spend a prescribed amount of time in the field interacting with customers on an ongoing basis. Train them to ask the right questions and to look for new ideas relating to your products or services.

Step Three—Ask The Right Questions

So you're face to face with customers; what questions do you ask? Naturally you want to know what level of quality they are seeking. How much will they pay? If the quality were improved how much more would customers pay? How quickly do customers need the product or service? What do they like about it? What do they dislike? How well have they been treated as customers? What more could be done to make their experience more pleasurable?

Marriott Hotels and Resorts, using extensive market research and asking the right questions, has been able to define increasingly narrow customer groups to serve. This has resulted in the development of different lodging concepts such as the Courtyard by Marriott as well as megahotels such as the Atlanta and New York Marriott Marquis. Additional research has led to the introduction of in-hotel services such as miniconference centers, executive business centers, video checkout, and concierge levels of service as well as one-stop planning and automated billing services for meeting planners.

An easy way to make certain the right questions are being asked is to trade places with the customer. If you were the customer what sort of things would you want the purveyor of the goods or services to know about the product?

Consider a brainstorming session with employees from the various aspects of your operation. The purpose is to compile a comprehensive list of questions that need to be answered with respect to customers' needs and desires. These questions can then be used by sales associates, customer service personnel, and market researchers during direct customer encounters.

At Cohen-Esrey Real Estate Services, Inc., we manage several thousand apartment units along with many other commercial real estate activities. Over the years we have boiled down the key questions that our apartment leasing consultants should ask prospective residents. These questions have been incorporated into a prospect information card that is completed for every customer. The card (see Figure 2.1) prompts the rental consultant to re- member to ask all of the basic questions that are critical to determining the customer's needs. Thus, not only does a company need to define the right questions, but it also must ensure that the questions are then asked of each customer.

Step Four—What Are The Customer's Alternatives?

To understand what makes your customers tick, you need to be aware of their alternatives. Where do they go if they don't buy your products or services? If you are the only game in town, can customers postpone their purchase? Is there competition? What are your competitors doing for their customers that you aren't doing for yours? NIKE, the wildly successful shoe company, takes pride in introducing services that no one else in the industry is providing. For example, its program, "NIKE Next Day," guarantees that an order called in before 7:00 P.M. Central Standard Time, will be delivered by 10:30 A.M. the next day via Federal Express. Orders called in by noon are shipped out the same day

FIGURE 2.1: Guest Card

COHEN•ESREY

GUEST CARD

	DATE SCHLD.	DATE COMPLD.	INITIALS
Call			
Tour			
Revisit			
Revisit			
Revisit			

PROSPECT NAME _____

CURRENT ADDRESS _____
_____

HOME PHONE _____ WORK PHONE _____

EMPLOYER _____

EMPLOYER LOCATION _____

MOVE-IN DATE _____ UNIT TYPE DESIRED _____

RENTAL BUDGET $ _____ APPROX. AGE _____ CHILDREN _____ PETS _____

WHO TO OCCUPY? _____ WHY MOVING _____

TRAFFIC SOURCE (Mark all that Apply):

NEWSPAPER AD ☐ (Which Paper?) _____ YELLOW PAGES ☐ APT. GUIDE ☐

DRIVE BY ☐ RESIDENT REFERRAL—CURRENT ☐ FORMER ☐ (Who?) _____

COMMUNITY REFERRAL ☐ OTHER _____

SPECIAL INTERESTS _____

PROSPECT GIFT _____ UNITS SHOWED _____

ADDITIONAL COMMENTS: _____
_____

TOUR ANALYSIS

Positive Features/Reactions　　　　　　　　Benefits

_____
_____
_____
_____
_____
_____
_____

Objections　　　　　　　　Solutions/Benefits

_____
_____
_____
_____

What will it take to close this prospect? _____
_____

before 6:00 P.M. And NIKE's 24-hour service desk enables it to take orders 24 hours a day, seven days a week.

How do your prices compare? Is there a discernible difference in quality? An electronics retailer in the Midwest advertises its "Secret Shopper" program. The company claims to have people continually shopping at competing electronics stores to determine pricing levels and product supply. If a lower price is found in another store the price is marked down accordingly.

Knowing what its competition could provide, Xerox undertook a detailed survey of United Airlines' copiers—500 machines in 300 locations. The survey included machine, service, and supply costs, complete with a comparison between Xerox and the competition. With an eye on the competition, Xerox proposed to oversee United Airlines' copier needs on a nationwide basis which helped make the difference in the signing of an order for nearly 600 new copiers. According to Xerox vice president, William F. Glavin, "We showed United how Xerox could save them money over the long term. That combined with reliable machines, service support, and our plan for nationwide monitoring won the business." By knowing the capabilities of their competition, Xerox was able to figure out how to provide products and services to meet the needs of the customer in a way that their competitors would find difficult to match.

Step Five—Dig Out More Facts

In addition to talking directly with your customers, roll up your sleeves and dig out more facts about them. Comprehensive market research isn't just limited to large corporations. While small firms may not have the funds to pay for sophisticated independent market research studies, there are many ways to get similar information on your own. Questionnaires can be sent to your customers and salespeople can be trained to ask certain questions and record responses.

Statistics may be boring to some but you could be missing a golden opportunity if you fail to sift through factual information on a regular basis. What is the age of your customers? Where do they live? Are they married? Male or female? What is their ethnic background? How much do they earn? Where do they work? How long have they been customers? One of the most important things to watch when looking at demographics and statistical data are trends. Not only do you need to know the composition of your customer base today, but you also need to know what it has been in the past and how it may be changing for tomorrow. With this information you can develop your own corporate strategy to meet the ever-changing needs of an ever-changing customer profile.

American Express, utilizing sophisticated computers, has created a customer profile on all of its cardholders, involving 450 factors such as age, marital status, sex, purchasing preferences, and so on. The company then uses the information to target its approach for selling its wide array of services and products. American Express not only believes that it makes sense to know all it can about its customers from a service perspective, but it also reduces marketing costs by avoiding attempts to sell products that aren't likely to be purchased by a particular consumer profile.

Marriott has used its market research to design hotels to meet the needs of handicapped and disabled citizens. Using customer feedback and operating experience, Marriott has championed accessibility features in all areas which the public must use. There are no raised thresholds. Ramps lead to all new restaurants and lounges. Drinking fountains and telephones are lowered. And access to public restrooms is typically through a series of buffer walls rather than doors.

Factfinding has proven profitable for the Toronto Dominion Bank in Cambridge, Ontario. Every Wednesday for approximately five hours, bank representatives set up shop in the St. Luke's Place Retirement Centre, enabling residents to do their banking on the premises. By bringing the bank to the customers, Toronto Dominion has captured a larger market share of the retirees at St. Luke's than they might otherwise have accomplished.

Step Six—Buyers Can Be Liars

On the one hand, you must listen to your customers; on the other hand, buyers can be liars. What customers may tell you isn't necessarily so. Still, you must listen. The trick is to try and understand what your customers want and need without getting bogged down in semantics. This can be accomplished by knowing as much as possible about each individual customer. A consumer may tell a salesperson that her budget permits her to only pay $250 for a new 35-mm camera. In fact, the $250 limit has been established arbitrarily by the customer and has nothing to do with her real needs. The savvy salesperson will skillfully ask more questions to find out more about this customer. The salesperson may learn that the customer's primary concern is not so much the price as it is finding a camera that is extremely durable. This particular customer is planning a mountain-climbing expedition and needs a camera that can be dropped and jostled and still do the job. Knowing this, the salesperson can then proceed to show different cameras that meet the customer's true needs. In the end, the customer may or may not pay more than $250, but at this point, the price factor may not be an issue.

An even simpler example of the buyers-are-liars theory occurs countless times every day. You walk into a clothing store and a salesperson approaches and asks, "May I help you?" The common response is, "Thank you, but I'm just looking." At this point, the salesperson wanders off, leaving you to "look" at your leisure. Maybe you are "just looking," but often this is just a way of telling a salesperson that while you intend to buy something, you don't want to be pressured. Instead of asking a closed-end question (one that can be answered with "yes" or "no"), the salesperson might instead introduce himself and start to establish a rapport with a question like, "Have you ever shopped in the ABC Clothing Store before?" This may be a disarming way to get to the point of finding out what customers really want and need as opposed to taking the chance that they will meet their own needs through the self-help "just-looking" method.

Step Seven—Be Creative

Be creative in attempting to know your customers. Suggestion boxes can be helpful in this respect and will be discussed later as part of quality control. How about forming an employee task force to tackle this challenge? Involving employees on a continuing basis can result in excellent feedback as well as indicating to them that their company cares about their ideas. Make sure the task force includes a number of employees who are on the firing line dealing directly with customers. The mission of the task force is to get employees to share their perceptions of what customers need and to dream up new ways to accomplish customer need determination.

Step Eight—Stir The Pot

As you learn more about your customers, do something. When you listen, hear, and understand, don't remain inert. Stir the pot—create activity. Incorporate the information you have gathered into your planning process and experiment with new techniques, products, and services. When something works, strive to improve on it with more customer research. Don't let all of the hard work that went into understanding your customers end up in someone's file drawer. By constantly analyzing what customers want and need, new products and services can be created.

Knowing your customers comes through walking around, asking questions, and listening to answers. It must be combined with careful and constant evaluation of empirical data. Both components are necessary to successfully provide products and services that meet customers' needs.

Action Plan

1. Resolve to make a concerted and consistent effort to get to know your customers.

2. Be a good listener. Don't impose your own beliefs or preferences on your customers.

3. Get down in the trenches. Have personal one-on-one encounters with your customers every single day.

4. Ask the right questions. find out how much customers will pay, what level of quality they desire, how quickly they need your products or services, and what they like or dislike about your product.

5. Know what your customers' alternatives are. Know who the competition is and shop it regularly.

6. Dig out more facts. Learn more about your customers through demographics and other factual data.

7. Buyers can be liars. Don't just listen to your customers but strive to understand their needs. This may require the use of subtle techniques to establish enough of a rapport to get your customers to open up and articulate their wants and desires.

8. Be creative. find new and innovative ways to get to know your customers.

9. Stir the pot. Don't let the information you have obtained gather dust. Use it to improve your products or services and to create new ones.

CHAPTER 3

Develop An Overall Customer Strategy

T here are countless businesses in this country that go with the flow where customer service is concerned. A lot of well-meaning people simply don't sit down and plan a customer service strategy. Instead, they do the best they can and react to situations as they arise. In some cases this approach is successful—in many instances it is not. A very small business with a handful of employees may be able to intuitively maintain a high degree of customer sensitivity without any sort of formal planning. But, as an organization grows beyond a few individuals it becomes much more difficult to maintain any sort of consistency in meeting customers' needs, unless a plan has been developed for this purpose.

Business managers at all levels must be involved in developing the customer service strategy. It is not enough for the CEO to mandate a customer service philosophy. Instead, the strategy must be developed by a team. Not only is the brainpower of many different people more productive than a single individual, but ideas emanating from a team are more likely to be accepted enthusiastically by all employees.

Planning and research are the cornerstone of a successful customer service strategy. The Metropolitan Life Insurance Company and a team of professors from Texas A&M University have been involved in research on service quality. Their results show significant differences between service and product quality.

They are also able to pinpoint what influences consumers' perception of quality service. Many internal factors that contribute to the service quality gap are things that can be controlled. A summary of the study, published in the Winter 1987 edition of *The Quality Review* (published by ASQC), identifies the fact that:

> Services are intangible—they cannot be measured, tested, or verified in advance of sales to assure quality. Services have a high labor content—they reflect the behavior of the service personnel who are intrinsic to service delivery.... The consumption of many services is inseparable from their production—and the customer often participates in the service delivery process. Finally services are perishable—they cannot be saved or inventoried. Once the opportunity is missed, there is no second chance to sell a service to a customer.

With this research, Metropolitan Life has been able to incorporate the findings into its internal planning process. All departments are requested to provide, as part of their annual planning objectives, an assessment of the gap that exists between customer expectations and perceived levels of service. Managers must explain how they will reduce this gap.

One of the best ways to accomplish the development of a customer service strategy is to form an employee task force as mentioned in Chapter 2. This task force should start with a clean slate and address every aspect of the customer service philosophy and how the company intends to operate. This philosophy must be transformed into a strategy for eventual implementation at all levels of the firm.

A customer service strategy is fluid and ever changing. It cannot be etched in stone forever. A successful approach to customer service involves evaluating what is working and what is not, and then constantly fine tuning the strategy. Thus, the task force will not only work toward an initial strategy, but should also monitor the ongoing aspects of the program.

Some of the topics that might be explored by the task force include the following.

Establish Quality Levels

Certain minimum acceptable standards for the delivery of products or services are needed. These standards should be clearly stated and quantified where possible. In a restaurant or a store, it may be decided that minimum acceptable standards will stipulate that there will never be more than three customers in line at one time to place their order or pay for their purchase. The Xerox Corporation has taken this a step further. Their "Leadership Through Quality" concept states that "whereas the conventional performance standard for quality is some acceptable level of defect or errors, the quality performance standard in Xerox is products and services that fully satisfy the requirements of our customers."

Consider A Credo

The task force may determine that a company credo is in order to reinforce the organization's philosophy for employees and the public. These credos can take the form of a "Customer's Bill of Rights," warranties, guarantees, and the like. In my company we have developed "Standards of Excellence" which are framed and hung on the walls in our corporate and regional offices as well as in the offices of the individual apartment properties we operate (see Figure 3.1). Minimum acceptable standards are published for all to see.

Training Is The Lifeblood

A customer service strategy must contemplate how employees will be trained and retrained to meet customers' needs. Once the desired level of quality has been established for products or services, employees must be trained to consistently produce accordingly. Not only does this involve training from a technical standpoint, but it also involves sensitizing the company team to the highest pinnacle of customer awareness.

FIGURE 3.1: Standards of Excellence

Cohen-Esrey Real Estate Services Inc.
Standards of Excellence

1. Staff—We intend to be helpful, polite and genuinely interested in serving your needs. We subscribe to the fundamental philosophy that the CUSTOMER is always right, and we will make very effort to make your residency here as comfortable and enjoyable as possible.

2. Maintenance—Our goal is to handle all requests for maintenance within 24 hours of receipt. If this cannot be accomplished, you will be advised of the status and expected completion date. We will leave your apartment clean and provide you with a written explanation of the work that has been completed in your apartment.

3. Common Areas—Hallways, lobbies and breezeways will be kept clean at all times. We will also replace light bulbs as soon as they burn out and monitor timers so that lights come on at the proper time.

4. Grounds—The grounds of this apartment community will be picked up daily to keep them free of trash and debris. In addition curbs will be swept regularly and kept free of leaves, grass clippings and other debris.

5. Parking Areas—We will keep parking areas free of trash. Abandoned vehicles will be tagged and removed quickly after they are identified. We will also have snow removed by 7:00 A.M. if snowfall occurs at night, and by 4:00 P.M. if snowfall occurs during the day.

6. Recreational Facilities—All facilities including swimming pools, tennis courts, clubhouse, laundry room, etc. will be kept clean and in good repair at all times. Swimming pools will be opened on or before June 1st of each year and the water will be kept clean and sanitary.

7. Apartment Preparation—We are committed to correctly preparing every apartment for occupancy including expert painting, cleaning and general maintenance and repairs. We will inspect your apartment with you prior to moving in to make certain you are 100% satisfied.

8. Quality Control—At least once each year we will distribute a quality control questionnaire to you asking for your suggestions and likes and dislikes about your apartment community. We also believe in an open-door policy and invite your comments and suggestions at any time.

9. Emergencies—We are available 24 hours a day, 365 days a year, for any emergencies that may occur. We will provide you with the means to contact personnel from our apartment community should an emergency occur.

If we should fail to keep our commitment to you and maintain these standards of excellence, I invite you to contact the Cohen-Esrey Corporate Office at (816) 531-8100, and express your concerns. If there is anything I can do to improve our service please feel free to let me know.

Signed: Robert E. Esrey, President

Johnson & Johnson, the makers of many health care products, uses the following statement.

FIGURE 3.2: Our Credo

OUR CREDO

We believe our first responsibility is to the doctors, nurses and patients, to mothers and fathers and all others who use our products and services. In meeting their needs everything we do must be of high quality. We must constantly strive to reduce our costs in order to maintain reasonable prices. Customers' orders must be serviced promptly and accurately. Our suppliers and distributors must have an opportunity to make a fair profit.

We are responsible to our employees, the men and women who work with us throughout the world. Everyone must be considered as an individual. We must respect their dignity and recognize their merit. They must have a sense of security in their jobs. Compensation must be fair and adequate, and working conditions clean, orderly and safe. We must be mindful of ways to help our employees fulfill their family responsibilities. Employees must feel free to make suggestions and complaints. There must be equal opportunity for employment, development and advancement for those qualified. We must provide competent management, and their actions must be just and ethical.

We are responsible to the communities in which we live and work and to the world community as well. We must be good citizens—support good works and charities and bear our fair share of taxes. We must encourage civic improvements and better health and education. We must maintain in good order the property we are privileged to use, protecting the environment and natural resources.

Our final responsibility is to our stockholders. Business must make a sound profit. We must experiment with new ideas. Research must be carried on, innovative programs developed and mistakes paid for. New equipment must be purchased, new facilities provided and new products launched. Reserves must be created to provide for adverse times. When we operate according to these principles, the stockholders should realize a fair return.

Johnson & Johnson

Implement Quality Control Measures

Quality assurance methods should be planned and implemented. Internally, the company must police itself to see that the minimum acceptable standards are met before products or services are ever delivered to consumers. Externally, ways should be developed for a company to test customers' reactions to products or services and learn whether or not customers' needs are being met.

Marketing Customer Service

The task force should address the packaging of customer service and utilize it as a marketing tool. When a company is doing it right and making the customer the king every time, there is nothing wrong with a little horn tooting. The customer service strategy could include a focus on how the company can market its quality and service philosophy to consumers and do so in an appropriate manner.

Plan For the Crisis

The corporate strategy should anticipate that crises do occur, no matter how well an organization functions. In such instances, how well the company remembers the customer is a true test of its customer service capabilities. If the customer takes a backseat to the typical CYA (Cover Your Assets) mentality that usually prevails, then the customer isn't really king after all. Planning for a crisis and putting the customer's best interests at heart are essential components of the overall customer service strategy.

Maintain Profitability

No one will deny that the reason for being in business is to make a profit. But if profits are the primary focus and customers are secondary, then priorities are mixed up. Instead, the strategy should be designed to put customers first in the most efficient way possible. If this simple concept is always maintained, then profits will flow. And, it is important that a company earn a profit so that it can remain capable of providing quality products or services. When corners are cut to enhance short-term profits, quality suffers and so do customers. Sounds like a chicken and egg thing, right? Clearly though, it all starts with meeting customers' needs.

Technology and Customer Service

There's no question that modern technology has become an integral part of our business world. Today, it's not whether computerization will be accepted in a particular business situation, but rather in what way and how well the computer application can enhance it. While it isn't mandatory to have computers and space-age technology to provide outstanding service, such tools can definitely benefit a customer service program. NIKE has invested millions of dollars in advanced state-of-the-art computer and warehousing systems. NIKE sales representatives carry portable computers and can check product availability on the spot. They can take orders and transmit them to the home office overnight. And the company is developing computer-to-computer capabilities for order processing, invoicing, shipping notification, and similar operations. Kodak recently spent $50 million to automate its distribution system and to purchase other equipment geared toward serving its customers more quickly and accurately than before.

Wal-Mart uses satellite technology and sophisticated computers to maintain inventory levels. How does this affect customer service? With precision inventory control, Wal-Mart is able to keep the proper number of products in stock so that they are available when needed by customers. And by not having too much or too little of each product, Wal-Mart keeps its inventory costs at the lowest possible level, passing the savings on to their customers.

At the insurance firm of Crum and Forster, electronic publishing and printing technology has been used to produce an automated insurance policy that is tailored to individual customers. The policy is easy to read and understand and enables consumers to be more at ease with their insurance policy.

Federal Express utilizes an advanced computer information system called COSMOS. Customer service is woven into this system, which stands for Customer Oriented Service and Management Operating System. The company also points out that *cosmos* is the Greek word meaning "order," the opposite of chaos. The COSMOS system tracks every package through the Federal Express system—from the origin station, through the hub, and on to the destination station. The information needed to accurately trace all packages is gathered by means of scanning a bar-coded label on each package. This information is matched within the computer to the appropriate airbill and is available instantly through the Customer Service Center. Federal Express proudly points to the fact that, "Unlike many other systems, COSMOS tracks packages—not paperwork."

Customers of the Spiegel Company can return merchandise that does not meet their needs in a most convenient fashion. At any time, day or night, customers simply dial a telephone number that automates the process. A synthesized voice prompts callers to press different number combinations based on information contained on the shipping forms. Thus, customers who come home from work and find a Spiegel shipment that isn't to their liking, can make a call at 11:00 at night if they choose, and, without talking to a soul, can arrange to have the order picked up by the company at a prescribed day and time.

Technological applications, as they relate to meeting consumers' needs, are numerous and permeate the product/service preparation and delivery process. Examples include the following:

1. Customer communication can be timely and accurate through the use of:
   - Modern telephone systems with multiple features.

- Mobile telephone and paging systems.
- Voice mail.
- Toll-free 800 numbers.
- Video cassettes.
- Audio cassettes.

2. Product ordering can be expedited through the use of:
   - Computer-to-computer hookups.
   - FAX machines (you can even order from restaurants using FAX machines).

3. Standardized production and quality assurance can be facilitated through the use of:
   - Computerized manufacturing equipment.
   - Robotics.

4. Customer profiles and need determination can be generated with assistance from:
   - Computerized tracking systems.

5. Product/service distribution can be handled with the use of:
   - Bar-code scanning systems.
   - Computer data transmission.
   - Modern jet aircraft, trucks, railroads, and ships.

6. Inventory control and invoicing can be maintained by using:
   - Computer-to-computer methods.
   - Satellite technology.

7. Tracking the competition can be accomplished by:
   - Computer-to-computer methods.
   - FAX transmissions.
   - Satellite technology.

Over the past 20 years, there has been literally an explosion of business hardware, software, and other technological advances that can be instrumental in providing quality service. Yet, it is important to remember that technology only broadens the base of customer service. As Dr. Anthony J. F. O'Reilly, president of food giant H. J. Heinz, points out, "When service reaches the point of sale, it must be personalized. Technology also permits such personalization as long as it is designed to conform to the requirements of the customer and not the other way around."

As a customer service strategy is created, a company must determine how technology and computers will be used to deliver service. There is no way to anticipate where this all may lead, but at least it initially enables an organization to know how to deploy such resources.

Shaping The Strategy Further

At Xerox, five critical factors have been identified to make Leadership Through Quality work and to increase corporate performance. With a focus on quality, the company is able to enjoy a reputation of solid customer service. The five critical factors that enable Xerox to succeed with its quality and service strategy include:

1. Complete commitment by senior management.
2. Top-down development and implementation.
3. Constant inspection by senior management.
4. Integration of the process into the day-to-day business.
5. Discipline and patience.

While all of these factors are important to the customer service strategy, Xerox's recognition that quality and service must start at the top of the organization is the key ingredient as it is with any business. This premise cannot be emphasized enough. Without the commitment of senior management, no customer service strategy can flourish as it must.

Federal Express has identified Strategic Objectives/Critical Success Factors. They include:

1. Achieve **100% service levels** on each and every transaction, including the related information concerning that transaction, in concert with our customers' expectations.

2. We must also continue to **improve the value** of our services to our customers.

3. Recognizing the pervasive requirements for high priority logistic systems in today's fast-paced economy, we are dedicated to **getting closer to our customers** in every way.

4. Recognizing that Federal Express is a creation of high technology in general, and the computer/microprocessor revolution specifically, we have based our strategy on the **substantial use of computer technology**.

5. The Company's strategy requires that we **produce a strong cash flow** and adequate profitability to continue our investments in systems that will meet our customers' future needs.

As you can see, these are broad and significant areas of inclusion. Developing strategies and programs requires considerable thought and discussion. Plan on regular meetings for the task force to continue to determine the effectiveness of the customer service strategy and how it should be improved. A clearly defined customer service strategy that is constantly communicated and understood by everyone in the organization is paramount to the ultimate goal of providing perfect quality products or services.

Action Plan

1. Avoid the tendency to go with the flow. Develop a specific strategy for providing customer service.

2. Create a task force of employees at all levels, including top-level management, to develop the strategy.

3. The strategy should address quality levels for all products or services.

4. Credos can be useful in reinforcing minimum acceptable standards of quality for both employees and consumers.

5. Training must be addressed as part of the strategy.

6. Explore quality control methods to be implemented to ensure that minimum acceptable standards are maintained.

7. Assume that your company is going to provide an enviable level of quality and service. Figure out ways to market customer service and toot your horn—but *only* if you have the track record to back it up.

8. Plan for a crisis and how you will care for customers when things go wrong.

9. Incorporate into the strategy methods for maintaining profitability with the understanding that customers come first.

10. Determine how you will use modern technology in your customer service approach. Remember that technology broadens the customer base, but at the point of sale, the encounter must be personalized.

11. A commitment by the CEO and top-level management to customer service and executing the strategy is critical.

12. Remember to continually communicate the customer service strategy to everyone in the organization.

CHAPTER 4

Training Is The Lifeblood

While in another city recently, to appease my children, I patronized a well-known national hamburger restaurant. I observed an occurrence that I believe is fairly common throughout the world in one form or another. There must have been 10 or 12 young employees working behind the counter. Only one smiled during the 20 minutes it took for us to wait in line to receive our order. It was 11:30 A.M.—the beginning of "crunch time" for this establishment, when it really gets busy. The order for the people in front of us was filled improperly—no one said "I'm sorry." A customer came to the counter and asked for barbecue sauce. "We're out of barbecue sauce," came the sour reply from the counter attendant. No explanation was given (I also wondered why they were out of the sauce at 11:30 A.M.). When we received our order it also was filled incorrectly. Why did all of this happen? The answer is simple—the employees were not adequately trained to handle "crunch time," and the restaurant manager was not properly supervising the staff.

Training is the lifeblood of a customer service philosophy. Training is performed to accomplish two primary objectives. The first is to provide quality products or services in the most efficient and profitable manner. The second is to instill a sense of customer awareness and sensitivity. In plain English, training can be defined as "teaching someone to do the job right the first time and to do so in a way that satisfies the customer."

Customer service really does begin with doing the job right the first time. Dr. Anthony J. F. O'Reilly, chief executive officer of H. J. Heinz, told this story about a driver making crucial deliveries using a rented truck with electrical problems.

> He calls the rental company and within an hour the truck is fixed. Additionally, the rental company representative stays with the driver for the next five hours to help him make deliveries and remain on schedule. This is a wonderful story. I commend the rental company employee for his diligent attention to his customer. But something is wrong with this picture. As good as this repair service was, the ideal would have been no need for repairs in the first place. If the truck had worked properly the first time, the customer would have been satisfied, and the rental company would have saved the cost of the repair. This, in turn, would benefit other customers since I assume the cost of extra repair work eventually got passed on to somebody else. Quality attained means service assured. One flows naturally from the other. And the way to attain the highest level of quality is to do everything right the *first* time.

"Do the right thing right the first time" is the motto for quality management according to Federal Express. Says James L. Barksdale, chief operating officer, "We've started a program of Quality Action teams...and have learned from them that success is seldom the result of a few big technological or conceptual breakthroughs, but rather, hundreds of small innovations and improvements throughout the organization." So how does one go about training employees to do it right the first time?

In the previous chapter we took a look at customer service strategy. After understanding the customers' needs, a company must establish standards by which these needs will be fulfilled. Such standards evolve into the pledges and credos that have already been discussed. Communicating the standards to each employee is the challenge that must be met by every company. This aspect of communication leads to the development of training programs. And, of course, thousands of training ideas have been generated by companies of all types and sizes throughout the country. To start the process, consider preparing job descriptions for each employee.

Job Descriptions

Job descriptions do not need to be so rigid that employees' activities are totally restricted. Instead, they should basically define employees' duties while remaining flexible enough to become more encompassing if necessary. Job descriptions should also provide enough latitude that employees can act with some degree of autonomy whenever appropriate. Finally, the customer service theme should be woven through every job description in clear and articulate terms. Nordstrom's, the Seattle-based department store chain, gives its employees the freedom to do just about anything to make customers happy. Stories abound of Nordstrom's employees who have gone above and beyond the call of duty to take care of their customers when they encounter out-of-the-ordinary circumstances. Without this flexibility built into their job descriptions, these employees might not be in positions where they could rise to the occasion for the benefit of the customer.

What might a customer-sensitive job description look like? A sample job description for a custodian in a high-rise apartment building is shown in Figure 4.1. The custodian is a front-line service provider who can make or break the residents' perception of the quality of life in their building. For this reason, it is imperative that the custodian have a thorough understanding of his or her role and its importance to the overall operation of the building.

With job descriptions in hand, a company can create training programs for its various employee groups. The first thing to remember about training is that it is and should be ever changing. Don't fall into a trap of developing a training concept and then sit back and think you are finished. Just as soon as you think you have everything established, something about your business will change and thus you will need to change your training approach.

FIGURE 4.1: Sample Job Description

Ajax Towers Apartments
Custodian's Job Description
For Mr. John Doe

<u>ALWAYS</u> SMILE AND GREET EVERY RESIDENT OR VISITOR YOU SEE; LOOK THEM IN THE EYE AND SPEAK THEIR NAME!!!

FREQUENCY	FUNCTION
Hourly	1. Empty ashtrays in lobby and at each elevator vestibule.
Daily	2. Vacuum hallways on floors one through six including dusting the baseboards. Carry a shampoo product in a small plastic bottle to clean spots on carpets as they are noticed.
Daily	3. Polish metal plating in elevator cars number one and two each morning. Carpet in elevator cabs to be vacuemed and spot cleaned.
Daily	4. Clean restrooms in lobby including sweeping, mopping, buffing, and waxing on same schedule as lobby floor. Also scrub toilets, sinks, and mirrors daily, stock paper products as needed and empty refuse containers.
Daily	5. Wash the inside and outside of lobby windows.
Daily	6. Vacuum office area and empty refuse container.
Daily	7. Clean laundry room including sweeping, mopping, buffing, and waxing on same schedule as lobby cleaning. Also, wipe off all machines, clean out lint traps, and empty refuse containers and ashtrays.
Daily	8. Sweep and wash front walk each morning.
Daily	9. Sweep and mop tile lobby floor.
Daily	10. Check and change burned-out light bulbs in office, lobby, laundry, restrooms, and hallways.
Weekly	11. Buff tile lobby floor on Monday, Wednesday, Friday mornings.
Monthly	12. Wax lobby floor on first Monday of each month.

REMEMBER, <u>ALWAYS</u> SMILE AND GREET EVERY RESIDENT OR VISITOR YOU SEE; LOOK THEM IN THE EYE AND SPEAK THEIR NAME!!!

Corporate "Universities"

Major companies spend millions of dollars each year training their employees. One of the most successful training programs has been shaped by McDonald's restaurants. They invested a small fortune in Hamburger University, a training complex located in the Chicago area. In 1983, the $40 million facility was opened complete with seven auditorium classrooms containing computer equipment for grading examinations, translation booths for foreign students, cooking equipment, and a variety of audiovisual aids. Hamburger University has the capacity for 750 students and offers courses that are university accredited.

From the book *McDonald's Behind the Arches* by John F. Love, we are told of Herman Petty, McDonald's first black franchisee, who employed nearly 500 workers at his Chicago restaurants, nearly all of them black. "Petty made certain that their first work experience was positive by investing heavily in training. He hired a woman with a master's degree in education as his full-time training instructor and opened a classroom in the basement of his third store. Because most job applicants are underprivileged, Petty's training goes beyond cooking hamburgers. 'Racial animosities are washed out of their heads,' Petty says. 'We train our people to realize that everyone is a human being and we all have to treat each other that way. We tell them what working is all about and where the money comes from. People who have worked here come back asking me to take on a younger brother or sister because they know they'll be trained well and will get respect.'"

Many other companies have intensive classroom training programs as well. The Chicago-based clothier, Hartmarx Corporation has recently established Hart Schaffner and Marx University for the purpose of training personnel to provide top-quality service. The first semester, in the spring of 1990, was 40% overbooked, as demand for the program was overwhelming. The L. L. Bean Company has a three-week training program, and Proctor and Gamble has a course for new employees that is in session for 40 hours a week over four to six weeks.

One underlying principle, the focus of most successful training programs, is that everyone is a human being and we all have to treat each other that way. It goes beyond the how-to of any business. James L. Barksdale of Federal Express says, "Basically we have discovered that if we treat our people with respect and dignity, they will provide a high level of service to our customers —whose business will yield profit for the corporation."

J. Willard Marriott once said, "Treat your employees the way you would like to be treated—provide them every avenue to success. Get their confidence and respect. Have them like and be interested in their job."

What is the best way to train employees to perform their tasks in a quality fashion while maintaining a high level of customer sensitivity? Obviously there are as many methods as there are companies. While large companies may have the financial resources to utilize expensive facilities and professional instruction, small companies can develop their own training programs at a much lower cost. A small company can divide the training function among its managers and structure its own curriculum using its own personnel.

Audiovisual Productions

The video and electronics explosion has spilled into employee training. Many firms are using professional video productions as major elements in their educational process. Federal Express uses Interactive Video Instruction combining the best in computer technology, along with audiovisual capabilities, to provide an excellent way for employees to train themselves. According to Federal Express, Interactive Video is the offspring of the 20th century's two most powerful technological innovations: computers and television. A high-speed microcomputer drives a laser video disc player that feeds full-motion video, graphics, and audio into a high-resolution color monitor. The user controls this medium through a touch-sensitive screen.

The system's greatest assets include its ability to:

- Train large numbers of employees in remote locations.
- Standardize information.
- Reduce training travel expense.
- Provide modeling and simulations.
- Provide real-time access to employee.
- Provide individualized and prescriptive instruction.
- Provide competency-based instruction.
- Increase learning retention.

The weaknesses are said to include:

- High development cost.
- High equipment cost.
- Lengthy development time.
- High cost associated with rolling out equipment.
- High cost associated with remastering and redistributing revised programs.
- Suitable primarily for curriculum where content is stable.

American Express has used video training to implement its Service Tracking Report (STR), a quality assurance concept. Wal-Mart has a satellite hookup from which it can beam training programs to locations throughout the country. The managers of McDonald's restaurants will leave training videotapes continuously playing in employee break areas.

In my company we videotape a series of monthly training sessions. Then, employees can check out the tapes if they wish to again study a particular area of our operation. In some cases, our management staff may assign the viewing of selected videotapes to employees who need to be retrained on a certain subject.

Besides videotapes, audiocassettes can also provide excellent, cost-effective training. Employees can listen to audiocassettes while driving in their automobiles, at home while cooking dinner, and in many other situations. The duplication of this medium is quite inexpensive. Audiocassettes can also be extremely versatile. For example, a major national trucking firm regularly produces audiocassettes for its drivers. They are then able to listen to the tapes while on the road. The tapes contain information about what is happening within the company, driving and safety tips, customer service hints, and other items of interest. Some companies are even experimenting with playing audiocassettes in the work place that contain subliminal messages. Soft music is heard consciously by the employees, but underlying voice dubbing conveys customer service affirmations to the subconscious mind of all listeners.

Seminars/Classroom Training

Classroom training and seminars are universally accepted training methods. In the commercial real estate business in which I am engaged, seminars presented by nationally known experts are usually attended for their training benefits. My firm holds monthly meetings for our apartment management personnel. We address many topics in a training format, utilizing role playing and small group discussions as two specific techniques. In one meeting we held our own version of the television game show "Family Feud." Apartment managers were pitted against each other in a contest to see who could correctly answer a series of questions involving our marketing and customer service training. It was a fun, lighthearted attempt at improving employee retention of the subject matter, and it appears to have been successful. In another instance we played our own version of "Wheel of Fortune," again querying the managers about our customer service philosophy. Feedback from participants in both events was extremely positive. Our people told us that they actually learned things they had missed in previous training sessions.

Written Manuals

Written manuals are probably one of the least effective training methods; however, such documents are generally necessary as a part of a total training effort. Manuals tend to be long and stuffy, and they become quickly outdated. An attempt should be made to streamline a training manual as much as possible. Training manuals that are a part of a classroom situation or seminar can be structured in an outline form where employees are able to take their own notes. Over the course of the seminar, employees will, in effect, create their own manual and will be highly likely to retain the information that was presented. Written manuals can also be helpful for future reference purposes when employees have specific questions. It might be appropriate to write the manual in such a way that it would actually become a series of manuals on specific subjects. In so doing, the manuals will probably be shorter and less intimidating to read then one large volume. Their value as future reference materials will increase, as they will be easy to use when they appear to be small and subject specific.

Continuing Education

Training should not be limited to new employees. Smart companies will engage in periodic retraining of existing employees. Such continuing education is based on several theories:

- People need to have concepts, methods, and techniques reinforced over time.

- New ideas and better ways of doing things can be introduced during continuing education sessions.

- Old and/or bad habits have a better chance of being discarded if employees hear how to do things the "right way" often enough.

Not only should internal continuing education be developed, but employees should be encouraged to obtain outside training as well. University courses, personal development classes, and a multitude of seminars are great places for eager employees to expand their knowledge. Corporate management may want to consider subsidizing the cost of such training, particularly in instances where the forum may enhance employees' ability to improve the quality of their work and their customer awareness.

Regardless of the medium, the components of a training program must be tailored to each particular situation. Some of the more common topics of instruction include:

- Telephone etiquette.
- The proper way to write a letter to a customer.
- The customer-sensitive manner in which to handle customer requests.
- General sales training.
- How to keep a positive frame of mind all day long.
- Dealing with unhappy (and sometimes rude) customers.
- How to conduct customer need determination.
- How to build a rapport with a customer.
- How to make the customer feel like a king without wasting time.

Additionally, a training curriculum should include a discussion about the company and what it stands for. This is the perfect time for the introduction of the customer service strategy and any company credos. Naturally the technical aspects of an employee's job will be a core part of the training. It is wise to also spend time educating employees about all aspects of the products or services provided by the firm so that they have a total understanding of what role their particular company plays in its industry.

Product/Service Knowledge

Isn't it frustrating to go into a store and ask a salesclerk about a particular product only to find out that this person knows less about it than you do? The only reason that this happens is because the salesclerk hasn't been educated about the basics of each product he or she is selling. How can the customer be properly served when the provider of a product or service doesn't know enough about it to begin with? Employees on the firing line must have product/service knowledge acquired through training. A good training program will include the demonstration of products with adequate employee participation. If store sales personnel are going to sell kitchen appliances, then they ought to use them to see how they work. What's more, once employees have firsthand knowledge regarding product performance, they will be better able to sell it with conviction to interested customers. Furthermore, having determined customers' needs, trained sales personnel will be better able to match the product with the need. Automobile dealers frequently allow salespeople to drive the cars they sell. While this is a nice perk, it also enables the salespeople to become comfortable with the product they are selling. Retail establishments should encourage their sales staffs to take products home and use them. Restaurants should require that waitresses and waiters sample different meals from the menu so they will be better informed when discussing the selections with their patrons.

Jump On The Bandwagon

The Gallup Organization conducted a survey for the American Society for Quality Control, which was released on October 3, 1989. A cross section of executives within the 1,000 largest corporations as listed by *Fortune* magazine were asked, "Are there specific quality education efforts under way in your company?" The responses are shown in Figure 4.2.

FIGURE 4.2: Are there specific quality education efforts under way in your company?

	Total %	Large Companies %	Small Companies %	Service Companies %	Industrial Companies %
Yes	82	89	74	78	88
No	18	11	26	22	12
Don't Know	*	*	0	0	0
Total	100	100	100	100	100
Number of Interviews	601	298	303	381	218

*Less than one-half of one percent.

More companies are realizing the benefit of formal training programs. Clearly, training is the lifeblood for a successful customer service program.

Action Plan

1. The primary emphasis for a company training program is getting the job done right the first time.

2. Written job descriptions should be prepared for each employee to help him or her understand the performance standards that are expected.

3. Job descriptions should also be flexible enough to allow employees the latitude necessary to meet customers' needs.

4. If the company is large enough, consider establishing a corporate university providing intensive ongoing training. If this is not feasible, look into participating with a company

that already has such a training facility or program or work with a local public university to develop specific training programs.

5. Video and audio productions can be cost-effective ways to provide employee training. If possible, continuously run training tapes in break rooms and other areas out of the public view.

6. Classroom and seminar training is similar to corporate universities, but on a smaller scale. Utilize existing staff to teach a carefully developed curriculum.

7. Streamline written manuals as much as possible. Use them as resource materials—don't rely on them to be the total training program. Attempt to structure them to be used in conjunction with classroom and seminar training.

8. Remember that continuing education can be beneficial to some of the "old hands" in the organization. Experienced employees need to be kept up to date on changes within the industry.

9. Give thought to what employees specifically need to be trained for. This will include everything from basic customer interaction and sales to the technical aspects of job functions.

10. Ensure that all salespeople have a thorough understanding of each product they are selling. Allow employees to personally use products whenever feasible to increase their familiarity and to show how products may be beneficial to customers.

CHAPTER 5

Do It Right
The First Time!

S o far we've talked about customer service being an attitude, understanding customers' needs, developing a customer service strategy, and training employees to be customer sensitive. In essence this is preparatory work for the real mission, and that is to deliver top-quality products or services at the most competitive price...and to do it right the first time! Everyone has heard the saying, "How do you have time to do something again if you didn't do it right the first time?"

Just how well do American-made products meet quality standards? That question was posed, by the Gallup Organization in the survey for the American Society for Quality Control, to executives within the 1,000 largest corporations listed by *Fortune* magazine. Specifically they were asked, "Thinking about the quality of American-made products today, if '1' means an exceptionally poor product and '10' an exceptionally good product, how, on a scale of 1 to 10, would you rate American-made products in general?" The results are shown in Figure 5.1.

Poor Quality Is Expensive

Inferior quality has a high price tag. It is expensive to correct mistakes. Labor, equipment, and capital must be redeployed to compensate for a company's losses resulting from product or service flaws. If two out of every 100 widgets manufactured are

FIGURE 5.1: How would you rate American-made products in general?

	1986	1987	1989	Change 87–89	Large Companies	Small Companies
	%	%	%	%	%	%
Rating						
10	3	2	1	−1	0	3
9	3	2	3	+1	1	3
8	23	18	22	+4	20	24
7	33	33	36	+3	38	34
6	17	24	20	−4	20	18
5	13	15	12	−3	14	11
4	4	4	3	−1	3	3
3	2	1	2	+1	2	2
2	1	*	*	0	0	*
1	*	0	*	0	0	1
Can't Say	1	1	1	0	2	1
Total	100	100	100	——	100	100
Number of Interviews	698	615	601		298	303

*Less than one-half of one percent.

imperfect, it reflects (theoretically) a 98% quality success ratio. Doesn't sound too bad. Let's also assume that the profit margin on each widget is 20%. This means that the manufacturer is foregoing the 20% profit on two out of every 100 widgets that are made, *and* is also absorbing the remaining 80% cost factor into the other 98 widgets. The cost to a company with annual sales of $100,000,000 is $1,600,000 in actual out-of-pocket manufacturing costs and $400,000 in lost profits. By improving the quality of the operation so that a 99% quality success ratio is achieved, the company can put another $1,000,000 on the bottom line. I don't know of many CEOs that wouldn't jump at the chance to do this if the cost to improve the quality is negligible. Many times the cost directly related to quality improvement also helps to enhance productivity in other ways. Thus, the cost to improve quality may not actually be a cost at all.

What does poor quality actually cost American companies in hard dollars? Experts estimate that defects can cost as much as 20% to 25% of gross sales. Service companies can spend 35% or more of their operating costs redoing things that weren't done right in the first place. These numbers are staggering. Rather than raise prices to generate high profits, a competitive firm should first look at reducing its costs resulting from defective products or inferior service. Think about it—if that same company with $100,000,000 annual sales mentioned in the previous paragraph actually had the industry average 20% defect rate, by totally eliminating this problem the firm could rake in an additional $20 million in profits!

Unfortunately, we have a tendency to accept errors and mistakes and their related costs rather than demand perfection every time. In an American Management Association Research Report entitled "Close to the Customer," a story is told about a midwestern purchasing agent:

"Let's make it tough on them," said the purchasing agent, writing out the specifications for the company's first order from a Japanese subcontractor. "On the ball bearings, let's accept no more than three defects in every ten thousand."

Tough it was, far more stringent than the rates allowed to American companies. And so it was with great excitement that the firm opened the Japanese shipment when it arrived. In each crate of ten thousand they found a letter:

Dear Sirs:

Enclosed please find the ball bearings you ordered.

We do not know why you wished to receive three defective bearings with every ten thousand, but we have enclosed them, wrapped separately and identified with crosshatchings so that you will not mistake them for good ones.

Diminished Credibility

Another price that a company pays for quality problems is its diminished credibility in the eyes of its customers. This is a more intangible factor and is often difficult to measure in dollars and cents. Research by the Technical Assistance Research Programs Institute from 1981 to 1986 provides some very eye-opening facts. Specifically, the negative word of mouth generated by dissatisfied customers is double the positive word of mouth spread by satisfied customers. Only 19% of customers with purchases over $100 will buy again from the same company if a complaint is not resolved, and 54% *will* buy again if the complaint is resolved. Is it worth the risk that errors in quality could potentially cost you more than 50% of those customers who receive defective products or services? What about the potential customers they tell?

In 1982, Xerox found that 92% of the parts flowing from its manufacturing sites worldwide were defect-free. There were two negative consequences of that 8% defect rate—cost and customer dissatisfaction, according to Robert L. Fletcher, manager, Material Quality Assurance.

> We estimated that paying people to inspect all those incoming parts to catch the bad ones and redoing all that work was costing us somewhere in the neighborhood of $75–100 million a year. And the longer a bad part stays in the system the more it costs us. You can imagine the potential cost if it gets into a machine that is eventually delivered to a customer and creates problems. Then we're talking about service time, annoyed customers and, in the worst cases, a customer who decides to take his business somewhere else.

Through a crusade to improve quality, Xerox was able to achieve a 99.5% quality target within five years and today boasts of a 99.95% defect-free rate. Chairman David T. Kearns says, "Four million parts a day go through our Webster [New York] facility. Each one-tenth of a percent defect rate on those parts costs us a half-million dollars a year." With these kinds of numbers, it's no wonder that Xerox has worked so hard to improve quality throughout its system.

Barbara Wold and Associates of Irvine, California, in a survey of retail customers, provides the following perspective:

Why Customers Quit

- Three percent move away.

- Five percent become involved in other friendships.

- Nine percent leave for competitive reason, e.g., more convenient location.

- Fourteen percent are dissatisfied with the product.

- Sixty-eight percent quit because of an attitude of indifference toward the customer by the owner, manager, or some employee.

Clearly, an indifferent attitude reflects a lack of quality within an organization.

Leonard L. Berry, past president of the American Marketing Association, said, "Service excellence is a never-ending journey; the only option is to plug away toward better quality every day of every week of every month of every year." There are a number of concepts that can work for companies of all sizes to enable them to "plug away" toward attaining their quality goals.

Quality Starts At The Top

Just as it is important to understand the consumer's need for quality on a continuing basis, top-level corporate management must also take a genuine interest in quality assurance. A periodic speech to the "troops" by the CEO doesn't quite get the job done.

Management, starting with the chairman of the board, must rub shoulders with the employees on the assembly line and behind the sales counter on a daily basis; more "management by walking around," as it has been termed. Management personnel must continually probe to find out how employees feel quality can be improved. By showing such an interest and implementing changes that make sense, management can build an esprit de corps among employees who will then strive to deliver 100% perfection.

J. Willard Marriott, founder of the Marriott hotel chain, was known for his "roll-up-the-sleeves" attitude in this regard. He believed that, "You exert a powerful, positive influence on your people and customers through your willingness to Set The Pace, Be Involved In Details and Follow Through. Your attention to little things can send a big message to the employees, telling them,...If these details are important enough for me to be concerned about, they're important enough for you to attend to as well." This philosophy is further exemplified through a couple of anecdotes from Marriott's illustrious career:

> In all the lounges where we have recessed lights, we should consider covering them with shields, like we have done in Atlanta, so that the bright lights don't shine directly on our guests.

> I suggested that they put more juice into the pan with the barbecue meat so that it would not be so dry, and use a perforated spoon to let the juice run out, and turn the barbecue over on the roll like we used to do. It would make a better barbecue.

Stanley C. Gault, CEO of Rubbermaid provides another example of how quality starts at the top of an organization. Gault is known to regularly visit stores and inspect his own products to determine their quality. If he finds a product that does not meet his standards, he purchases it from the store, and returns to his office to find out why it was inferior and how it left the plant in the first place.

Training Is Still The Best Bet

There is no question that training tops the list in terms of programs that a company can implement to ensure that quality prevails. Quality starts with the premise that employees must know the expected standard for end products or services and how to get there step-by-step. Without adequate training, it is very difficult for employees to understand quality requirements and the process to accomplish them. Truly, as discussed in the previous chapter, training is the lifeblood for producing quality goods and services.

Employee Recognition For Quality

Assuming that a comprehensive training program is in place, the next step is to develop an employee recognition system for those who perform in an outstanding fashion to promote the quality and customer service concepts. This can be accomplished through cash remuneration, trips, plaques, and other awards. Some will ask, "Why should we reward employees for just doing a job the way it is supposed to be done?" This is a valid argument however, the key is to incorporate such rewards into the overall compensation program. Very simply, employees should be hired with the understanding that they can earn a salary at one level for meeting minimum benchmark quality standards and at a greater level for attaining higher benchmarks. In addition to individual awards, consider developing similar means of recognition for groups of employees to promote a team approach.

Federal Express has a multitude of programs to recognize its employees for exemplary service. A Hall of Fame focuses on the top salespeople each year and the Golden Falcon award is presented to couriers and customer service agents who "go above and beyond to meet our customer's needs." A Bravo Zulu award, named for the Navy's signal for "well done," enables a manager to give quick cash, a dinner, or similar prize to any employee who has performed in a particularly outstanding manner.

American Express has Quality Awareness Month with $23,000 in awards going to individuals who are top performers. Special recognition goes to members of the Super Quality Club where work units have performance levels of 100% for four months or 99% for five months. The Quality Employee of the Month program allows department managers to select one individual as being most outstanding in quality achievement. Recipients are bestowed with a private luncheon, certificates, and T-shirts.

At Cohen-Esrey Real Estate Services Inc., we utilize a variety of quality recognition methods. On a monthly basis, a Property of the Month Award is presented to the on-site management team that has excelled in the overall operation of an apartment community—a large part of the criteria centers on quality and customer service. In addition to a plaque that is placed in the apartment office for all to see, the name of the property is added to a master plaque that is displayed in the Cohen-Esrey Corporate Office. President Robert E. Esrey writes a letter of congratulations to the staff, a copy of which is forwarded to the client who owns the property. Annually, a Hands-On Property Management Award is won by two employees who have consistently demonstrated their dedication to quality service throughout the year. Plaques and gift bonds are the tangible result.

Employee recognition should be contemplated for more than just individuals. Whenever possible, employees should be recognized as a team. Successful organizations are learning the benefits of getting personnel to function as a team instead of as a collection of lone rangers. The Japanese epitomize the team approach and have found that it increases productivity and quality. Teamwork can be structured whereby individual members can specialize in providing a service or function to the team, or employees can rotate responsibilities so that everyone eventually performs each task. America West Airlines has used the latter approach where ground personnel rotate between working at the ticket counter, on the reservations desk, and as baggage handlers. This concept promotes versatility and employees are less likely to become bored. At the same time, the demand for outstanding training is heightened.

Where teams are utilized, recognize the achievements of the team and not the individuals. If cash remuneration is involved, each team member should receive his or her share. If plaques or certificates are awarded, there should be one for each team member, and it should clearly identify the individual as a part of the team. Avoid singling out one member of the team for recognition.

Job Security And Company Pride

Besides awards and compensation, management can further strive for quality and customer service by creating a new atmosphere of pride for its employees. People will take pride in their work (and quality will improve) when they feel that they are appreciated by their employer. Job security is a primary concern to most employees. Smart managers are finding ways to ensure job security in this age of merger mania where the axe is falling on thousands of workers in the name of corporate belt tightening. At Federal Express a decision was made in 1986 to discontinue electronic mail service. Over 1,300 employees were affected by this change in policy, but no one lost a job. The company reorganized and kept virtually every person in the work force. Chief operating officer Clarence Barksdale says, "Basically, we have discovered that if we treat our people with respect and dignity, they will provide a high level of service to our customers."

Wal-Mart shares a similar philosophy. Founder Sam Walton implemented a simple but powerful corporate theme entitled, "We Care." This concept extends not only to Wal-Mart customers, but to its employees as well. Except they aren't called employees, but instead are "associates." The words "we, us, and our" have helped build a mutual respect held by management, salesclerks, and warehouse staff that has made Wal-Mart one of the most proud and service-oriented companies in America.

Reduce Employee Turnover

Reducing employee turnover can help to build quality. Each time new employees are hired, a company must make an investment in their training. Additionally, all new employees have a learning curve during which the propensity for error is greater than normal. When turnover is reduced, the corporate machine has a better chance to hum along and produce at optimum levels.

Employee turnover can be reduced in a number of ways, starting with hiring the right person to begin with. Care must be taken to see that job candidates are properly screened and tested, if necessary, for compatibility with the prospective task. Hiring the right person is not an easy task. Look for prospective employees who appear to be intuitively customer service oriented. Check past job references and inquire specifically about how employees measure up in delivering quality products or services. Evaluate the prospect's demeanor: Is he or she genuinely outgoing and comfortable as a people person? During the interview process ask a question from time to time that may reflect the prospect's personal beliefs about quality and service.

Subtlety is the key, because many people role play very well during interviews and may tell you what they think you want to hear. For example, someone applying for a sales position might be asked, "What is the first thing you do during a customer encounter?" The response you are hoping for is, "I would greet the customer in a warm and friendly manner and attempt to establish a rapport." You might even invite prospective employees to actually demonstrate their response instead of just answering the question. Prospects could also be asked how they might go about determining customers' needs. Ask prospects to tell you what they consider to be the final act with the customer. You want to know if, as employees, they will follow up to see if customers are satisfied.

Once hired, proper training is paramount. The recognition factor previously mentioned becomes of prime importance. Employees want to feel as though they are appreciated and that what they are doing makes a difference. In-depth job counseling for problem employees should be provided in an attempt to salvage them and make them productive team members. If this internal evaluation uncovers personal problems that are being brought to the work place, employees should be redirected to obtain professional help if warranted.

A safe and cheerful working environment will improve employee morale and help to reduce turnover. In high-risk industries, extra care must be taken by top-level management to see that the health and well being of employees is protected. Employees should be made aware of the company's commitment to this objective.

Interestingly, studies show that financial compensation is not the most important factor to American workers. In fact, depending upon the study, employee recognition, a sense of accomplishment, and job security can rank higher than the paycheck. Still, no one likes to feel that they are being taken advantage of and a competitive wage will send a signal that the company does value its team members.

Avoid Complacency

While reducing employee turnover, care must be taken not to fall into the trap of complacency. The same employees performing the same functions day after day can lead to complacency and quality can slip. We all have experienced becoming absorbed in our thoughts and at the same time continuing to go through the motions of whatever we are doing at the moment. It happens to me at times when I'm driving and following a route I take regularly. I get so caught up in my own thoughts that I go right past my destination. The mechanical aspect of driving the car and the familiarity of the route are so comfortable that I tend to switch my mind into a different mode and fail to pay attention to where I'm going. Unfortunately this can happen so easily with work functions, and mistakes can be made that lead to product and service problems. Complacency can be combated with job rotation, continuing education, and periodically changing and improving the work environment.

Capital Equipment Expenditures

In the manufacturing sector, defect-free production can be further enhanced with state-of-the-art equipment. When factory equipment malfunctions due to age, obsolescence, or maintenance practices, the possibility exists that production quality may decline. Corporate budgets should contemplate ongoing expenditures for replacing, retrofitting, or overhauling capital equipment. Xerox has recently cut overhead in the factory through a major financial commitment to automation that is now saving the company nearly $500 million annually. More companies need to take the cue from Xerox. In most cases the funds are seldom wasted when used to upgrade plants and equipment in order to produce a high-quality product at low costs. This is an excellent way to meet the expectations of today's consumers and the challenge of foreign competition.

Control Over Suppliers

The quality of suppliers' materials and services is critical to the quality of the overall product or service. It's like the saying about computers—garbage in, garbage out. If poor-quality materials or design flaws are incorporated into the production process, this becomes the weak link in the chain. Chances are that the final product won't meet quality standards. One of the most tragic examples of this was the disaster of the space shuttle *Challenger* in 1986, when seven brave astronauts lost their lives in an explosion seconds after lift-off. During the ensuing investigation it was discovered that a pressure seal failed due to a faulty design. Because one small component of the huge and complex shuttle system was inferior, the entire spacecraft was obliterated and lives were unnecessarily lost.

The same care given to the quality assurance of a company's products or services should also be given to monitoring the quality of the materials and components used to make those products. Suppliers must be notified as to the minimum standards that will be acceptable for their materials. The Wal-Mart organization is a leader in this area, having a reputation for being very tough with suppliers, in terms both of price and quality. A company has every right to demand quality from its suppliers and must take the necessary measures to see that quality is delivered consistently. A review of a supplier's quality control methods and overall success rate *before* commencing a relationship can help to weed out those suppliers who might become the weak link.

100% Perfection—The Only Goal

The American Society for Quality Control makes these observations about settling for anything less than 100% perfection. These were contributed by John G. DeMaria of the IBM Corporation in "What you get if 99% is good enough."

99%

In terms of services that most people view as essential, consider what you would get if people you depend on performed right only 99% of the time.

- At least 200,000 wrong drug prescriptions each year.
- Unsafe drinking water four days each year.
- No electricity, water, or heat for about 15 minutes each day.
- No telephone service or television transmission for nearly 15 minutes each day.
- Newspapers not delivered four times each year.
- Nine misspelled words on every page of a magazine.

So you see, the only acceptable target for companies to aim for is to produce products and services that are defect-free 100% of the time.

Which Method Is Best?

In the previously referenced Gallup Organization poll for the American Society for Quality Control, 601 executives were asked, "There are many ways to improve quality in general throughout American business. Using a 10-point scale, please rate the following in terms of importance, with '10' meaning it is a very important way to improve quality and '1' meaning it is not important at all."

Rating	Employee Motivation	Actively Involved Corp. Leader	Employee Education	Process Control	Quality Improve Teams	Expend. On Capital Equip.	More Control Over Suppliers	Improved Admin. Support Group Output	More Inspection
	%	%	%	%	%	%	%	%	%
10	44	46	39	21	17	10	11	10	10
9	19	15	21	11	11	9	7	6	6
8	23	24	24	27	27	25	23	18	13
7	9	7	11	18	18	21	19	16	15
6	2	4	3	8	8	11	13	14	12
5	2	2	2	9	11	16	17	22	17
4	1	*	0	1	2	4	3	5	6
3	*	1	*	1	2	2	3	3	9
2	*	0	*	1	1	1	2	2	6
1	0	*	*	*	1	0	1	2	5
Don't Know	*	1	0	3	2	1	1	2	1
Total	100	100	100	100	100	100	100	100	100

Number of Interviews = 601
*Less than one-half of one percent.

Action Plan

1. Poor quality is expensive. Recognize that in a manufacturing industry, inferior or defective products can equal 20% to 25% of gross sales.

2. Recognize that quality problems result in diminished credibility for a company in the eyes of unhappy customers.

3. Aim for 100% perfection and nothing less. Any level of quality short of this will mean extra costs and potentially dissatisfied customers.

4. Quality starts at the top of the organization. The president and other top-level management must be dedicated to quality. They must rub shoulders daily with employees and customers to make certain that quality standards are understood and met.

5. Training is the lifeblood. The chances of realizing 100% perfection are much better when employees are adequately trained.

6. The recognition of employees who achieve quality is integral to customer service and can take the form of cash compensation, plaques, newsletter features, and the like.

7. Teamwork should be promoted whenever possible. When a team produces desirable results, all members of the team should be recognized.

8. Job security and company pride will give employees additional incentives to work toward the goal of total quality.

9. Concerted attempts should be made to reduce employee turnover to heighten quality. This avoids the learning curve that is present with new employees, where there is a great chance for mistakes to be made.

10. Avoid employee complacency, which can lead to errors. Rotate job functions, make positive changes in the work

environment, and emphasize continuing education to guard against complacency.

11. Plan for capital expenditures to keep plant and equipment in state-of-the-art form. Malfunctioning equipment can contribute to defective products.

12. Exercise tough control over suppliers to guarantee that quality materials will be provided for use in manufacturing products. Don't let a supplier be the weak link in the chain.

CHAPTER 6

How To Tell If
You're Doing It Right

H ow can we tell if we're doing it right the first time? How do we measure quality? Who does it? Quality assurance methods must be developed. Internal testing measures are part of the process, but beyond that—ask the customer!

Before products leave the factory they should be inspected in some manner. Product testing can be performed at the factory where certain products are selected at random and examined in every conceivable way. Products are heated, cooled, blown, bombarded, crushed, stretched, scanned, dismantled, and so on. Likewise before services are rendered, care must be taken to ensure that they are delivered at acceptable quality levels. It's a good idea to review customers' needs in an ongoing manner and to measure services offered against customer expectations.

Once it has been decided that the products or services are ready to deliver, the focus shifts to monitoring customer reaction. There are scores of creative ways to accomplish this, but it is important to do more than pay lip service. I'm sure you have seen comment cards on your table at a restaurant. Have you ever filled one out? Was it because you were really unhappy with the food or service? Maybe the service was so spectacular that you completed the card to compliment the individual who was waiting on you. In either case, the response would have been based on an extreme reaction—terrible or incredible. What about the masses of people who experienced a reaction in between? They generally don't bother filling out such cards. Is the restaurant management getting a true picture of how their product and service are being viewed by the majority of their customers? Probably not.

Get Involved

While comment cards can be part of a quality assurance program, a much more active approach must be taken to determine whether or not customers' needs are being met. In restaurants, besides using the comment cards, what would happen if managers personally visited customers during or after meals and in a genuine fashion asked if the food was prepared satisfactorily and if the service was excellent? I've eaten at restaurants where it was obvious that the manager was paying attention to such details. This person was conspicuous in the dining room and was actively involved in seeing that service was superb. In an unobtrusive way, the manager would find the right moment to come by my table and warmly greet me by name and ask if the food was prepared just to my liking. As we left, he helped my wife with her coat and again asked if we enjoyed our dinner. I always leave such places with a good feeling about the meticulous concern that has been expressed over my satisfaction. Do I go back to such restaurants? You bet!

My theory about the responsibilities of CEOs may be a bit controversial in corporate circles. I believe that it is the primary and singular responsibility of CEOs to determine whether or not customers are satisfied. Certainly setting corporate goals and strategies is an important function of CEOs and the attainment of such objectives must be reviewed and evaluated through reports, charts, meetings, and the like. Too often CEOs and other upper-level management are insulated from customers and try to run the company from behind a desk. Many administrative and corporate functions can and should be delegated more than they are.

Smart CEOs and upper-level managers will spend as much time as possible out in the field. They will devote their energies to walking through the plant, store, or office talking with employees.

They will listen carefully to what is being said about problems in manufacturing operations. They will probe into the manner in which the company is delivering products and services. They will continually solicit customer reactions and look for better ways to get the job done. CEOs and managers will become extremely intuitive as to whether or not the proper level of quality is being attained. They will be constant cheerleaders for quality and customer service. At Ore-Ida, famous for its potato products, president Gerry Herrick periodically approaches employees and asks them to recite the company credo. When they do, they receive a cash prize.

For years, Motorola, Inc., had enjoyed a healthy growth, but distributors began warning management that the marketplace was changing and the Japanese were making inroads. As part of a process to retool the company, chairman Robert W. Galvin started a more formal program of customer visits. Galvin himself spent more time traveling to see Motorola customers, as did other members of the management team. The approach was simple, with two basic questions being asked: What do you like about Motorola, and what don't you like? Such visits were so productive that they have become a permanent part of the company's operation and have extended to all corporate officers. The quality of Motorola's products improved dramatically, and in 1988, the company was a winner of the Malcolm Baldrige National Quality Award, presented by President Reagan.

The Hyatt Regency Hotel organization has an annual event where members of corporate management spend time performing tasks normally handled by its employees. During 1989 the president of the company spent time as a doorman at one of the hotels in Chicago. A humbling experience? Not really, considering the fact that Mr. Hartley-Leonard was able to directly interact with customers who did not know who he was and observe their reaction to their overall experience with his hotel.

Managers should spend time doing the jobs of others to get an overall perspective as to how their company operates. I'm not suggesting that a nonpilot CEO of an airline should attempt to fly a jetliner, but he or she could work as a flight attendant for a day. Upper-level management of a restaurant chain could flip burgers for a day every now and then, and corporate officers of a retail department store could spend time at the checkout counter. Not only do such encounters provide management with a great level of appreciation for what their employees do to earn a paycheck, but these encounters are opportunities to rub shoulders with the customers.

Point of Purchase Surveys

A common method used to invite customer feedback is the use of point of purchase surveys. Usually this takes the form of a questionnaire card that is given to customers at the time they purchase products or services. Often this card is packed with the product. Point of purchase questionnaire cards are a bit impersonal and consequently offer minimal effectiveness. They *should* be a part of the total customer input strategy, as they do give customers opportunities to react to very positive or very negative experiences. Such questionnaires should be short and easy to complete. Include several questions that can be answered by marking a "Yes" or "No" box, or utilize some sort of grading system. Avoid asking customers a number of questions that require narrative responses. There should, however, be ample room for customers to write any comments.

One of the best comment cards I have seen is the "Report Card" used by the Days Inn motel chain. The questionnaire commences with a short statement from the firm's president, which is followed by a series of questions that can be answered using a grading system. Figure 6.1 shows how the card is structured.

There are varying opinions on who in the corporate hierarchy should receive point of purchase questionnaires. Many companies provide for their return to the CEO by configuring the questionnaire as a mailing piece. If this is to be done, a manager who is truly sensitive to customer satisfaction will see that the

FIGURE 6.1: Report Card

Welcome!

We are pleased to be your host and sincerely appreciate the opportunity to be of service.

We promise our guests a convenient, clean, attractive, and secure place to stay with friendly, attentive service at a fair price. It is very important to us that we do things right for you.

Only you can determine if we are successful. Please take a few minutes to let us know what we are doing well and where we need to improve.

On behalf of all the employees and owners in the Days Inn Family - Thank you!

Michael A. Leven
President and Chief Operating Officer
Days Inns of America, Inc.

Date of Stay_____ Room # _____

	Excellent				Poor
	A	B	C	D	F
1. Front Desk:					
Friendliness/Courtesy	___	___	___	___	___
Speed/Efficiency	___	___	___	___	___
Wake-up call/Messages	___	___	___	___	___
Reservations Efficiency	___	___	___	___	___
2. Your Room:					
Cleanliness	___	___	___	___	___
Attractiveness	___	___	___	___	___
Carpet Condition	___	___	___	___	___
Furniture	___	___	___	___	___
Bedding	___	___	___	___	___
Television	___	___	___	___	___
Heating/Air	___	___	___	___	___
Price	___	___	___	___	___
3. Your Bathroom:					
Cleanliness	___	___	___	___	___
Working Condition	___	___	___	___	___
4. Other facilities:					
Pool	___	___	___	___	___
Parking/Grounds	___	___	___	___	___
Public Restrooms	___	___	___	___	___
5. Restaurant:					
Cleanliness	___	___	___	___	___
Food Quality	___	___	___	___	___
Service	___	___	___	___	___
6. Overall rating	___	___	___	___	___

7. Would you stay at a Days Inn again?   Yes: [　]   Maybe [　]   No [　]

Additional Comments:

OPTIONAL:

Guest Name _____

Address _____

mailer is postage-paid. Recently I conducted an informal survey and collected comment cards from 10 different businesses. Three of them were not self-mailers, but instead the customer was expected to leave the card at the business establishment. Of the seven that were self-mailers, only two were postage-paid. I wonder how many customers will really bother to put a postage stamp on such a questionnaire? Does the company that fails to provide a postage-paid self-mailer really care whether or not customers respond?

Another type of point of purchase survey, usually applicable to a retail operation, is done personally by either the owner/manager or someone hired for this purpose. Customers who have completed purchases are approached and asked a few short questions to determine whether their shopping experience was acceptable. Customer interviews can be much more personal than comment cards and can be used in tandem. Also, the cross section of responses will be great because of the random nature of the approach.

Regardless of the method used, point of purchase surveys should be acknowledged by someone in the company—preferably by the CEO. How many times have you completed a comment card because you were unhappy with a product or service, and no one ever responded? Does the company really have a customer awareness, or is it simply going through the motions? A short note from the CEO or an upper-level manager goes a long way in demonstrating that the customer is king. In late 1989 I stayed at a Marriott hotel and completed a questionnaire card that was in the room. Frankly, the room and the hotel, in general, did not meet the high standards usually associated with Marriott. Shortly thereafter I received a personal note from Bill Marriott, the chairman of the board and president. See Figure 6.2.

While I haven't had the opportunity to stay there since, I did walk through the hotel a few weeks after receiving Marriott's letter. I noticed that the items I had noted on the questionnaire card regarding the corridors and common areas had been attended to.

FIGURE 6.2: Marriott's response.

Dear Mr. Harris:

Thank you for your comments about our Houston Marriott Brookhollow. I always appreciate hearing from our guests. It helps me keep in touch with how well we are measuring up to your expectations.

I am forwarding your evaluation to our General Manager concerning the problems you had with the cleaning and serving of your room and the other problems you mentioned. I am very disturbed to receive reports such as yours indicating we have "dropped the ball." Please be assured we will make every effort to follow up on your concerns.

Thank you for giving us the opportunity to serve you and for sharing your dissatisfaction with us. We look forward to your continuing to select Marriott Hotels as you travel.

Sincerely,

J. W. Marriott, Jr.

Customer Questionnaires

A technique very similar to point of purchase surveys is the use of questionnaires mailed to the customer. Again, postage-paid response envelopes are included and the configuration of the questionnaire is very similar to that of the comment card previously discussed. This type of questionnaire can be very useful to firms that may be providing ongoing services. In my

commercial real estate business, we periodically send questionnaires to our apartment residents and commercial tenants to see
how they feel about their building and if the level of service is
meeting their needs. We generally receive a response from 25% to
30% of the residents and tenants surveyed. In each case, we write
a personal letter thanking respondents for their comments, and we
specifically mention what we intend to do about any suggestions
or requests they have made.

Follow-Up Telephone Calls

Still another way to determine customer satisfaction is through
follow-up telephone calls. Though a very basic technique, the
follow-up call can promote excellent public relations as well as
provide valuable information. Many companies use telephone
surveys as an inexpensive component of their customer feedback
program. The Goodyear Tire and Rubber Company places a great
deal of emphasis on telephone contacts to solicit complaints about
their products. Gallery Furniture, a Houston firm that supposedly
generates more than $33 million in annual sales from a single
store, requires its personnel, upon completion of a delivery, to ask
to use the customer's telephone. The delivery person then calls the
store and reports to the owner, Mack McIngvale, his wife, or to the
operations manager that the delivery has been made. The customer
is then asked to come to the telephone where he or she is queried
as to his or her level of satisfaction with the merchandise and
service.

Employees initiating the calls must be trained not to sound too
"canned" with their questions and must be highly personable when
speaking with customers. CEOs and upper-level management
should participate in making such calls on a regular basis. Not
only does this keep them in touch with customers, but think how
much mileage the company can get when customers realize that a
busy corporate executive has taken the time to make such a call.
What would you do if Lee Iaccoca called you to ask how you like

the new Chrysler automobile that you recently purchased? You would probably tell 100 of your friends about this positive experience, thus enhancing Chrysler's public image.

Anonymous Shopping

Service-oriented companies can benefit from the use of anonymous shoppers. This can work for banks, hotels, restaurants, retail stores, and a host of other businesses. The concept involves having people pose as customers to make purchases from particular establishments. These individuals have been carefully trained to evaluate many aspects of their encounter and to provide reports on their findings to corporate management. In our commercial real estate business we send shoppers to our apartment communities to observe the marketing and customer service techniques of our on-site managers as well as the overall appearance of our product.

Here is still another area for active involvement on the part of the CEO and other managers, especially in large companies. The president of an airline can periodically fly in his or her own planes, the CEO of a major restaurant chain can eat in his or her own restaurants, and the corporate officers of a financial institution can make transactions at various branches, all with the purpose of finding out how well quality service is being delivered by their respective organizations.

Toll-Free 800 Numbers

Large companies with customers spread across the country or around the world may find it beneficial to provide toll-free 800 numbers for their customers. The use of such numbers varies greatly. In some cases customers may be calling for assistance about a particular product and in other instances to register a complaint or request general information. Training is exceptionally important for customer representatives who provide 800 number service. I was talking with a friend recently who had a credit card stolen. He immediately called the credit card company to report the theft and had the unfortunate experience of talking with someone who could barely speak English. The company representative was uninformed as to the replacement process and did not project a sympathetic attitude toward my friend, who was understandably frustrated and distraught over the incident.

At Resorts Condominiums International, the director of customer service makes lottery calls to his company's 800 numbers. The service representative who answers the telephone first receives $25. No one knows when such calls will be made.

Toll-free 800 numbers also tend to measure extreme reactions on the part of customers since it is the customers who must act to make the call. Sometimes, however, the results of 800 numbers can be surprising. The K-Mart Corporation reports that 47% of all calls on its Customer Care Network toll-free number are to offer compliments about products or services. General Electric has developed the GE Answer Center. It is intended to build a professional dialogue between consumers and GE as well as provide consumers with helpful information and expertise. The company believes that it also helps to build consumer confidence in GE. Representatives can answer a wide variety of questions about 120 product lines, 8,500 product models, and about 1,100 different procedures. GE utilizes a state-of-the-art telephone automatic call distributor, the largest available today, to handle over 3 million calls each year. It has been so successful that the U.S. Office of Consumer Affairs and *Fortune* magazine have designated the GE Answer Center as the leading, state-of-the-art customer service operation in the United States.

CEOs and corporate managers at all levels should become involved in answering toll-free 800 numbers. One day each month, David Kearns, CEO of the Xerox Corporation, spends time answering phone calls from customers. The duty is rotated among the company's other top officers as well. What better way to roll up your sleeves and stay in touch with customers?

Customer Group Encounters

A somewhat novel way to find out what is on customers' minds is to establish a group forum. Customers are invited to attend a small group discussion led by a management team member. This moderator asks a series of tough to-the-point questions about the firm's performance and asks customer participants to comment. In some cases it may be beneficial to have other managers attend to observe and ask questions. Naturally the forum must be such that the customers do not feel threatened, but instead will feel free to be candid and outspoken. A skillful moderator will be able to coax the group into focusing on the various issues and generate helpful suggestions that can be used for quality enhancement. The customers who consent to such an encounter could be rewarded at the end of the session for their assistance.

With our apartment management operation we periodically hold resident panel discussions during our monthly managers meetings. A cross section of residents from our various properties are asked about how well we are meeting their needs. The on-site managers also have an opportunity to ask their own questions of the panel. At first we wondered if we were opening Pandora's box, but the results have been extremely helpful. We generally let the chips fall where they may, which has been an eye-opening experience for many of our employees.

Again, it should be stressed that the CEO and upper-level management should be active in customer group encounters. For all of the reasons previously discussed, a CEO should often moderate such discussions. Additionally, with the permission of the customer participants, the forum should be videotaped.

Customer Service Departments

All companies can enjoy the benefits of a customer service department, even if it only consists of one person. The consumer affairs department can serve as a valuable link between customers and all levels of an organization. A customer service department does more than just receive complaints. Many of the customer feedback techniques that have been explored can be administered through such a department. Constant training of customer service representatives is absolutely critical. Not only must these employees have a thorough knowledge and understanding of their company's products and services, but they also need a depth of understanding and caring in order to deal with the countless different personalities that they are exposed to daily.

In the Winter 1987 *The Quality Review* (published by the American Society for Quality Control), John Condon, vice president of corporate quality assurance for Abbott Laboratories, wrote a memorable article for the "Cues: Commentary by the American Society for Quality Control" column. His observations should be the premise on which the modern customer service department is based. Condon wrote about his encounters with retail establishments:

> Occasionally, when I know approximately what I want, the clerk isn't familiar with that piece, so I wind up waiting for Charlie, who will be back in the proverbial five minutes.

> It didn't used to be that way. Not back in Mt. Vernon, Ohio, when I worked as a stockboy after school. There were no pop quizzes when you walked into Grant Smith's hardware store. Grant and his son-in-law Fred Seibold were professional hardware clerks. They knew the total business. In the course of the day they saw both housewives asking for whatchamacallits and tradesmen who knew precisely what they wanted. They listened to every customer and helped each find a solution.

> Grant and Fred not only knew their business, but they knew their products—and what those products could and couldn't do. They were matchmakers,

matching the customer's desired outcome with their products. You told them what you were trying to do, and they fixed you up with the right stuff to get it done.

Never once did you (the customer) ever have to know anything technical. You didn't even have to know what you needed. Grant and Fred figured that was their job. You could even come back in the middle of a project and get more advice on what to do next.

Sure, it took longer to respond to every customer and give him individualized attention. But from my vantage point back in the stockroom, I saw the same people coming back again, time after time, year after year.

Today's customer service departments should emulate the Grants and Freds of yesteryear. Customers should be able to call or come to a business and deal with company representatives who are unflappable and unwavering in their dedication to helping customers meet any and every challenge. When they don't have the answer immediately, they should find out and follow up.

Unfortunately many of us haven't seen very many of the Grant or Fred type of customer service representatives. A few years ago, however, I did have the privilege of dealing with one such individual in, of all places, the public sector. I was attempting to assist my mother in straightening out a rather complex Social Security matter and spoke with Bob Goldstraw, a service representative for the Social Security Administration. Not only was he a pleasure to talk to on the telephone, but when he didn't have the information I was seeking, he said that he would personally get the answer for me and call me back. Usually, one gets shuffled off to another department in such situations. The next day Mr. Goldstraw called me promptly as he said he would with the solution to my problem. I was so impressed with the attitude and performance of this public servant that I wrote a letter of commendation to the commissioner of the Social Security Administration.

Benchmarking

Competitive benchmarking is a concept whereby products and services are measured against industry leaders with a goal of achieving superiority in quality. Xerox is one of many companies that has effectively used benchmarking to meet its targets. These are customer satisfaction, cost, reliability, product development time, and return on assets. The firm benchmarks against the industry leader in every function, including AT&T and Hewlett-Packard on research and product development, L. L. Bean on distribution, American Express on collections, and American Hospital Supply on automated inventory control.

A practical example of benchmarking can be found at the local doughnut shop. The proprietor goes to the other shops in town and purchases a sampling of doughnuts from each. While there, he notes such items as the level of cleanliness in each store, the length of time it takes to be served, the attitude of the counterperson, and the variety and availability of selection. With the doughnuts purchased from his competitors, the proprietor conducts a test of the various products. He invites some of his customers to participate in a taste test where they eat doughnuts from his and the other stores. The proprietor carefully records the comments of his customers with respect to taste, price, and other factors.

Once his research is completed, he is then in a position to begin the benchmarking process. Assuming that he wants his store to be known for the highest quality and best value in the market, he compares his doughnuts in terms of taste (as perceived by his customers), price, level of service, and availability with those of his competitors. He accomplishes this by creating a matrix and a rating system similar to that shown in Figure 6.3. A rating of "10" is the highest and "1" the lowest. In reality, a much more comprehensive and sophisticated matrix would be established; however, this example has been simplified for demonstration purposes.

The proprietor can see that Competitor C rates slightly higher in total score and specifically in the areas of service and availability.

FIGURE 6.3: Doughnut Shop Ratings Matrix

Category	Subject Store	Competitor A	Competitor B	Competitor C
Taste	10	9	7	10
Price	8	6	9	8
Cleanliness	10	9	7	10
Service	9	5	8	10
Availability	9	10	6	10
Total	46	39	37	48

FIGURE 6.4: Does your company do competitive benchmarking?

	Total %	Large Companies %	Small Companies %	Service Companies %	Industrial Companies %
Yes	70	83	58	66	76
No	29	16	41	33	22
Don't Know	1	1	1	1	2
Total	100	100	100	100	100
Number of Interviews	601	298	303	381	218

(Interviews were conducted of a cross section of executives from 1,000 of the largest companies listed by *Fortune* magazine. The survey was released October 3, 1989.)

He gathers his staff and brainstorms ways to improve in both areas to equal or surpass Competitor C. Every three months he repeats this benchmarking process to make certain that he is meeting his goal to operate the top doughnut store in his market area.

How widely accepted has benchmarking become as a means for determining quality levels? The Gallup Organization's survey for the American Society for Quality Control asked the question, "Does your company do competitive benchmarking?" The answers are given in Figure 6.4.

What Happens To The Customer Feedback?

Soliciting and receiving customer feedback is only half the battle. What really counts is how the information is handled. The American Management Association conducted a survey of 267 companies in 1986. It discovered that reports of customer feedback by consumer affairs departments went to only 14% of company presidents or CEOs; 14% to a vice president of marketing; 7% to a vice president of consumer affairs; and 37% to other vice presidents. The most surprising statistic is that only 14% of CEOs received such information! How can a corporate customer service philosophy thrive and permeate an organization when the top executive doesn't know what his or her customers are saying about products or services.

Customer comments, suggestions and complaints *must* be forwarded to the CEO as well as be disseminated through the ranks. If the CEO and upper-level management are actively involved in finding out what the customer is thinking, then they will be the first to demand that all feedback received be provided to them.

American Express is a great example of a company that utilizes customer data in a comprehensive and sophisticated fashion. The firm has developed the Service Tracking Report (STR), a system with many functions and purposes:

- It shows results in terms of each service measured and tracks performance against local standards.

- It is a tool for identifying service problems and issues.

- It provides details of action programs.

- It disseminates practical solutions to service problems experienced by operations' locations around the world.

According to Mary Anne E. Rasmussen, vice president of worldwide quality assurance for Travel Related Services, the STR is "far more than a measurement system, but it is grounded in reams of facts." STR measures 100 different aspects of the American Express operation, including the speed with which emergency replacement of credit cards occurs, whether or not application processing time has increased, specific details on any problem that has occurred and what actions were taken to correct the problem, and the identification of methods to deal with common situations that are encountered throughout the American Express system.

The chairman of American Express, Jim Robinson, reviews the STR as does management in all American Express locations. The company also holds weekly executive quality results meetings. The senior vice president in charge of the service center assembles his or her operating and staff executives and discusses the most recent quality performance results. Says Jay W. Spechler, director of performance engineering at the Southern Regional Operations Center, "This is a hard ball, no holds barred event. Any executive whose department's performance is below 98% explains what went wrong and what the corrective actions for the next period are."

The company that wants to be a leader in customer service will take an aggressive approach to utilizing customer feedback. Point of purchase survey responses will be carefully tabulated and responses will be made as appropriate. The same will be true for customer questionnaires, follow-up telephone calls, and toll-free

800 number calls. Not only will the data be compiled, but it will be used by the CEO, upper-level management, and personnel throughout the organization. Furthermore, systems will be implemented that will ensure that every single customer request is resolved promptly, cheerfully, and 100% to the customer's satisfaction. Businesses cannot afford to fail to respond. A customer complaint or request is a chance for a company to sell itself. If it succeeds, it will have a chance to earn more business from customers and everyone else they tell. If it fails, the chances are good that customers will be lost along with the potential business of everyone else they tell.

The results from anonymous and CEO manager shopping, as well as on-site inspections, must be shared in a constructive and educational manner with the parties involved. And the information derived should also be shared with others, without singling out or embarrassing anyone, so that similar mistakes can be avoided—or in positive circumstances, so that other employees can learn of something that works. Videotapes from customer group encounters should be viewed by all employees for training purposes, so that all personnel can hear firsthand what customers think about a company's products or services.

Action Plan

1. Get involved! CEOs, upper-level management, and employees at all levels must take active roles in determining whether quality services or products are provided that meet customers' needs.

2. Incorporate point of purchase surveys including comment cards and personal interviews, as part of the customer feedback strategies.

3. Use customer questionnaires and respond promptly to requests and suggestions.

4. Make follow-up telephone calls to determine customer satisfaction. The CEO and other managers should get involved.

5. Anonymously shop your organization to get specific feedback, and if your operation is large enough, do the shopping yourself. Put yourself in the customer's shoes.

6. Establish customer group encounters to hear firsthand what is liked and disliked about your company.

7. Create a customer service department even if it is only one person. See that this department is dedicated to knowing everything there is to know about your products or services. Train customer service representatives to have total empathy for customers.

8. Identify companies that are leaders in your industry and utilize competitive benchmarking procedures to try to attain superior quality.

9. Do something with the feedback that you receive. Make sure that the CEO, all members of the management team, and all employees, where appropriate, receive the results of the feedback.

10. Follow up and make certain that every customer request is handled immediately and to the 100% total satisfaction of the customer.

11. Remember, a customer complaint or request is another opportunity to "sell" your company to the customer and to everyone he or she comes in contact with. Use such opportunities to build your business.

CHAPTER 7

If You've Got It
...Sell It!

T here is no question that companies with strong customer awareness have a decided competitive advantage in today's marketplace. Historically, the 1940s and 1950s comprised the age of simple and straightforward customer service. Things began to change in the 1960s and 1970s to the point that convenience overshadowed customer service. Everything (or so it seems) has become self-service. We pump our own gasoline at the gas station (it's no longer a "service" station); we serve ourselves at buffet lines in restaurants or receive our food at the counter of a fast-food franchise; we sack or box our purchases in many grocery stores; every business has a drive-up window; and there are more vending machines than ever before. Yet the pendulum may be swinging the other way as we enter the 1990s.

I believe that people are stepping back a pace and are scratching their heads, trying to decide if ultraconvenience is their primary desire. Consumers are more sophisticated than they were in the 1940s and 1950s. Not only do they want convenience at the lowest possible cost, but they also want quality with the best possible service. What a combination! Yet, it's easy to see why this has occurred. Foreign nations (using many of our technological discoveries) have made huge strides in their manufacturing capabilities. As a result of our long-standing free trade policies, many foreign companies are able to sell their products in the United States at a cost far lower than that offered by our own manufacturers. Thus, consumers have gotten used to, and expect, competitive pricing with every purchase they make.

It's an obvious fact that our life-styles have changed dramatically over the past 50 years. We spend more and save less than before. We want to live the good life. There are two working adults in more households than in the past. We're a go-go society and we want things quickly—we don't like to wait. The need for convenience is here to stay.

During the 1980s, however, we have had time to contemplate inexpensive convenient products and services. Many of us have been a part of the "Me" generation and we're realizing that there's more to life than our own self-interest. As this metamorphosis occurs, we're becoming tired of surliness at the checkout stand and finding that our inexpensive convenient products don't work as well as we expected. While we don't want to give up competitive pricing and convenience, we also want quality and service with a smile. Companies that can figure out how to successfully blend all four of these ingredients will be the blue-chip winners during the 1990s and beyond.

Package And Sell It

If your company has been able to achieve new heights in providing quality products or services with a maximum level of customer sensitivity, why not package and sell the concept? A number of companies are starting to do this, and sometimes in such effectively subtle ways that we don't even know that it's happening. There are some who believe that if they are providing quality and customer service, they don't need to hype this fact with a lot of marketing fanfare. They may be right to some extent. At the same time, the marketing and advertising of products and services have become complex and sophisticated. There are techniques that can provide a great deal of public exposure for a firm's quality and service, while still making it appear to be a low-profile company. We have all seen the Northwestern Mutual Insurance Company's advertising campaign portraying it as the "quiet company." It depicts itself as quietly doing business one customer at a time while inferring that its competitors are more concerned about being big and highly visible.

Don't Be Hasty

Before attempting to package and sell your customer service philosophies, make certain that you don't have any gaping holes in your program. If you have recently implemented new systems to ensure and monitor quality, wait to brag until you have a trend of steady results. Likewise, if you pride yourself in a customer service strategy, make certain it is running smoothly before blowing your horn about it. It is also a good idea to measure your quality and service levels against your industry in general. You certainly don't want to be promoting your company as a leader in these areas when, in fact, you are outpaced by your competitors. If you have suffered a terrible image in the past where customer relations are concerned, wait until you have turned things around and have a solid track record to talk about. Remember, credibility is the key to developing a marketing focus on your firm's consumer awareness prowess.

Consumer Education Materials

It can be said that some companies write the book on quality and customer service in their particular industry. There is more truth to this than might meet the eye. If you are an industry leader—small or large company—you undoubtedly have some unique business concepts that set you apart from the competition. You may be in a position to tell consumers what they should expect from companies in your industry. Why not go ahead and write a book on this very subject for distribution to your customers? Consumer education materials can be one of those subtle ways to let the public know that you genuinely care about their well being.

In our company, we are considered as a leader in maintaining top-quality apartments, office buildings, shopping centers, and industrial facilities. We pamper our commercial tenants and apartment residents to a greater extent than anyone else in the markets we serve. We are in the process of writing consumer education pamphlets that will be distributed to prospective tenants and residents outlining what they should expect from a landlord, whether it be our firm or another. We are covering such things as how quickly they should expect to receive maintenance service when they report a problem, the condition their commercial space or apartment should be in when they take occupancy, what their property should look like from an appearance standpoint on a daily basis, and how quickly they can expect to have their security deposit refunded after they vacate. The information will be factual and written in a public service fashion, yet there will be no mistaking that it is our company that is advocating such standards.

The Goodyear Tire and Rubber Company publishes a pamphlet entitled "How To Take Care of Your Tires." It's a 20-page, easy-to-read document that discusses tire inflation, tire rotation, wheel balancing, vehicle alignment, tire wear, replacement, maintenance, and driving habits. Not once is the Goodyear name mentioned, except in fine print on the back cover. It's obvious that this material is not a direct pitch to buy tires from Goodyear, and yet customers who are given the booklet at a Goodyear Service Center will know full well who is responsible for its publication and distribution.

The Coca-Cola Company has taken a different approach with its pamphlet, "How To Talk to a Company and Get Action." Published in 1982 by the Coca-Cola Information Center, this booklet has nothing to do with soft drink products. Instead, it concentrates on a consumer awareness theme. Here's how it starts:

Where do you turn for answers when you are looking for information to help you use a product or service better? For example, where would you go if:

- You or a family member is on a diet and you need to find out how many calories are in a serving of a particular food product?
- You have small children and you would like help in 'child proofing' your medicine cabinet or storage chest?
- You are fighting high electricity bills and would like to know more about the energy efficiency of various appliances?
- You would like to reduce your time in the kitchen and are looking for new cooking methods or other ways to use the food products you buy?

Similarly, when you experience a problem with a product you have purchased or a service you use, where do you go to get the problem resolved?

The pamphlet provides explanations on how to locate the company and the right person within that company. It offers advice on getting quick solutions to problems, provides industry sources, and describes the function of the Better Business Bureau. Readers of this publication can't help but come away with the feeling that Coca-Cola is on the side of the little guy.

Many other companies have prepared similar materials for use by consumers. Some have even gone so far as to financially underwrite consumer information services that are operated as cooperative public/private ventures. Do companies market such goodwill? Unquestionably, though in varying degrees. We've all seen television, newspaper, and magazine advertisements by businesses that encourage the consumer to "write or call for a free pamphlet," featuring a specific public service. Corporate sponsorship of consumer affairs seminars is usually prominently heralded in mass media formats.

While there is certainly an element of charitable spirit when Corporate America provides consumer education materials and forums, you can bet that a company will do its best to cultivate its image to the greatest extent possible. Its ultimate goal is to wrap itself in a warm, fuzzy "We Care About You, The Customer" blanket.

A word of caution is in order. Make certain that there is a balance between public service and pure commercialism. Consumers aren't stupid and will see right through a company's effort to polish its image if such an effort crosses the line with too much ballyhoo and horn tooting. When preparing consumer education materials, downplay the company just as Goodyear and Coca-Cola have done with their pamphlets. Remain modest and humble when highlighting your company's generosity through marketing and advertising campaigns. Select a subject for consumer education that is truly needed and in the public's best interest. Educate your own employees as to the contents of the materials you are producing and how they can participate in the subtle marketing of your concept. One-on-one employee/customer encounters can be quite productive in this respect.

Warranties And Guarantees

If you are truly producing top-quality products or services why not guarantee them? Lots of companies do and enhance their reputation for quality in the process. You should know, however, that in this day and age of consumer activism, things have changed where product warranties are concerned. People are paying attention to the conditions of warranties and even compare them from one product to another as they shop. You had better be prepared to perform where your warranty is concerned or the chances are good that you'll be dragged into court and lose. With all of the consumer watchdog agencies that now exist, you'll also face a lynch mob of governmental consumer affairs departments and attorneys general offices. If that's not enough, the press will have a field day informing the public that your warranty is a sham.

Once the risks have been weighed, the development of a warranty program can become a powerful marketing tool. The company that has become truly fanatical about quality and does it right the first time has very little down side when it makes such guarantees. Obviously the more comprehensive the warranty, the more appealing products or services may be to the buying public, especially if the competition is unable to do the same. The automobile manufacturers have one of the highest profiles when it comes to warranties, each one trying to outdo the others in terms of length and scope. We now see seven years and 70,000 miles as a benchmark—considerably higher than levels offered in the past. One company advertises that it guarantees the entire vehicle while its competitors only stand behind certain components. Midas Muffler guarantees its exhaust systems "for as long as you own your car."

In the manufacturing sector either a product works right or it doesn't. It gets trickier in the service industry. During 1989, both the First Interstate Bank and the Wells Fargo Bank (California) began a program where they paid their customers $5 if they stood in line more than five minutes waiting for service. Seattle's Sea First Bank had the same idea and was averaging $7,605 in payments each month for its 169 branches. Some restaurants offer diners total satisfaction with their meal or they won't be charged. Because of the subjective nature of such offers, a restaurant must be extremely confident that it can serve a meal that will be acceptable to even the finickiest of eaters.

Also in 1989, the Hampton Inn Hotels (formerly an independently operated subsidiary of the Holiday Inn chain) introduced the "100% Satisfaction Guarantee" at its 208 locations. Hampton Inns designed the program to give it an edge on the competition. It tested its guarantee in 24 hotels for 105 days and found that only one tenth of 1% of its customers asked for their money back. Interestingly, 96% of those who received a refund said they would try Hampton Inns again because of the guarantee. Through a good electronic tracking system the company can keep tabs on which of its guests invoke the guarantee, helping to minimize cheating.

Money-back offers can aid the stimulation of further quality improvements. Employees in the factory, in the office, or on the sales floor must be trained to understand the company's challenge to the public that it intends to sell a perfect product every time. And, from the customers' perspective, if they feel that businesses have dealt with them fairly and courteously, they may be less prone to exercise their warranty rights if products don't perform quite to their more subjective expectations.

When customers aren't satisfied, products or services should be replaced or refunds made in the most expeditious manner possible. The process should be hassle-free. Consumers should not be subjected to suspicious questioning or endure the third-degree treatment. Corporate management should view the incident as an opportunity for further fine tuning of its quality objectives, as well as the cementing of long-term customer relationships. Warranty claims should be carefully tracked and brought to the attention of the CEO and all other applicable employees.

Quality Institutes

Consider creating a quality institute for the purpose of providing public service and consumer awareness. Name the institute after your company and use it to dispense public information pamphlets, to conduct quality and service surveys, to donate books and tapes to area libraries, to underwrite public seminars on quality and service, and for any other suitable use.

Through a quality institute a company could work with local high schools and colleges to sponsor an essay contest. Students could write and submit essays entitled, "What Quality Means to Me." A panel of employees would read the essays and select the best entries. The quality institute could then award college scholarships to the winners. These stipends could range anywhere from as little as the payment of tuition for a semester at a local university to a full four-year all-expenses paid grant.

Involving young people in a quality campaign can be beneficial to the community and quite productive from a public relations standpoint. Executives of the 1,000 largest companies listed by *Fortune* magazine responded to the Gallup Organization survey for the American Society for Quality Control. The results from the question, "How would you grade the U.S. education system in terms of preparing new employees to do high-quality work?" are shown below.

Grade	Total 1986 %	Total 1989 %	Change %	Large Companies %	Small Companies %	Service Companies %	Industrial Companies %
A	3	2	−1	*	3	2	1
B	19	11	−8	7	14	12	7
C	46	43	−3	44	43	45	40
D	22	32	+10	35	30	29	37
F	9	12	+3	14	10	11	15
Don't Know	1	*	−1	*	*	1	0
Total	100	100		100	100	100	100
Number of Interviews	698	601		298	303	381	218

*Less than one-half of one percent.

There is no question that more needs to be done to improve our country's formal education system to better address quality and customer service. Private quality institutes can help to fill this gap.

Another idea worthy of further study is an intern program. College students could be hired through the quality institute to conduct quality assurance surveys, work as summer or weekend salesclerks (with comprehensive training in service and quality), make customer follow-up phone calls, and perform a variety of other service-related functions. It's entirely possible that some of these interns and scholarship winners could return as permanent employees in the years ahead. What a great way to start grooming the next generation for quality consciousness!

Media Publicity

When it comes to horn tooting, don't hesitate to use the local media. If your company has taken significant steps to improve quality or to utilize an unusual service concept, it may be worthy of coverage. Certainly the formation of a quality institute is a news item, especially if your company is making a sizeable financial endowment to get it launched. Essay contests, scholarship awards, and intern programs could receive major publicity. It may be necessary to write your own press releases (or to hire an advertising agency to assist you) containing the facts about the subject matter you wish to promote. Be careful not to be too self-serving. If the press release appears to be too much like a commercial for your firm, it may be passed on to the advertising department.

Direct Marketing

There are countless ways to directly market a company's quality and customer awareness. The only limitation is the creativity of the human mind. Let me share some packaging ideas that we use in our firm that I believe are illustrative of the direct marketing concept for all businesses. As I have said before, our company is a commercial real estate organization, and a part of our business is managing several thousand apartment units. Generally, in the past, the apartment industry has not done a great deal to market customer service. It seems as though we have always performed a number of services that are taken for granted by our residents.

We decided to formalize these services, enhance them to some degree, and sell them to the public. We created a program called Personal Plus Concierge Services, which was tailored to the resident profile of each of our apartment communities. Personal Plus may consist of as many as 14 different services, including dry cleaning pick-up and delivery in our apartment clubhouses. (We made arrangements with a local dry cleaner for this purpose.) We also pick up the mail and newspapers and water the plants for residents who are out of town, sell postage stamps in our apartment offices, detail residents' cars in the parking lots (again, we made arrangements with a local company), provide firewood supply for apartments with fireplaces, and provide a host of other services.

Parts of the program are free, and others are at cost with no markup. We also went to local merchants and obtained their participation in the program through discount coupons for purchases at their stores and businesses. We developed a Personal Plus logo, and brochures were printed explaining the different program benefits. We then trained our on-site staffs to sell the concept to existing and prospective residents. Brochures continue to be distributed to anyone who comes close to our properties, and we even take them into the neighborhoods and leave them with local merchants. It's been gratifying to see how the on-site management teams have taken this idea to heart. They are continually dreaming up new services and variations to the program that make it even more appealing for their customers.

We went a step further and formulated a new slogan, "Your Personal Service Assured by Cohen-Esrey Real Estate Services Inc." This was incorporated into our printed advertising and signage. Large round buttons were made emblazoned with the letters "YPSA" and worn by managers, leasing consultants, maintenance technicians, custodians, groundspeople, and other employees. Some of my partners felt that the slogan was too corny, but corny or not it's been catchy for the employees and the public. People are always stopping our personnel and asking them what YPSA means and then receive a pride-filled explanation. Employees have told us that when they tell people who their employer is, they commonly hear, "Oh, that's the personal service company." In one apartment community where the locks were rekeyed, a maintenance technician volunteered to stay into the evening to deliver keys to those residents who were not available to receive them during the day. He said, "That's what personal service is all about."

The point is that we have taken our services and packaged them in an orderly fashion for marketing purposes. In the process, we have become identified as a service-oriented company (a trait not often associated with landlords). Our employees have started looking for ways to go above and beyond the call of duty to exemplify Personal Plus and YPSA.

The use of slogans and mottos incorporating a company's commitment to quality and customer service can be a real asset when the company is clearly able to follow through and perform. The Ford Motor Company boasts "Quality Is Job 1." Grocer Albertson's, Inc., based in Boise, Idaho, touts "50 years of Quality Service and Savings." The cover of the Xerox Corporation's 1988 annual report simply states, "In both our businesses, customer satisfaction is the key to our success." Trans World Airlines ran a television commercial in which the pitchman told the audience that he and others fly the airline regularly to observe the quality of service and report directly to the chairman of the company. The list goes on.

Newsletters

A quality newsletter has been tried by several companies. American Express uses internal newsletters, video employee interviews, and special bulletins to heighten customer awareness. A regular quality newsletter can be an inexpensive marketing tool. It can include articles on how the company is tirelessly striving to improve its quality and sell error-free products or services. Employees can be featured who have provided exemplary customer service or who have won company service awards. Such a newsletter can serve dual purposes. First, as an internal publication, it can be a positive motivator for everyone comprised by the corporate family. Second, when mailed or given to customers, a newsletter can subtly demonstrate the degree of importance that a company places on quality and service. It exudes a company pride that is infectious with customers.

When packaging and selling standards of quality and service, credibility and consistency are paramount. A company must make good on its claims or its marketing efforts will fall on deaf ears. Employees should be challenged on a daily basis to safeguard the standards, for now, the company is publicly pronouncing a leadership role in the industry. Bring on the consumer advocates because the organization *will* perform!

The Malcolm Baldrige National Quality Award

No discussion of quality and customer service is complete without spending a few moments reviewing the Malcolm Baldrige National Quality Award, honoring the late Malcolm Baldrige, the 26th Secretary of Commerce.

Public Law 100–107, the Malcolm Baldrige National Quality Improvement Act of 1987, signed by President Reagan on August 20, 1987, established an annual U.S. National Quality Award. The purpose of the award is to promote quality awareness, recognize quality achievements of U.S. companies, and publicize successful quality strategies. The Secretary of Commerce and the National Institute of Standards and Technology (NIST) are responsible for developing and administering the awards, with cooperation and financial support from the private sector.

As many as two awards may be given each year in each of three categories: (1) manufacturing companies or subsidiaries; (2) service companies or subsidiaries; and (3) small businesses. The first awards were presented by President Reagan in November 1988.

Businesses incorporated and located in the United States may apply for the awards. Eligible subsidiaries are defined as divisions or business units of larger companies. Small companies are those with 25 to 500 full-time employees.

Seven areas are examined: (1) Corporate quality leadership, (2) Information and analysis, (3) Planning, (4) Human resource utilization, (5) Quality assurance of products and services, (6) Quality improvement results, and (7) Customer satisfaction.

Heavy emphasis is placed on quality achievement and improvement as demonstrated through quantitative data furnished by applicants.

Each written application is reviewed by three examiners. High-scoring applicants are selected as finalists and must undergo a site-verification visit by one or more examiner teams. A panel of judges reviews all data and information and recommends award recipients. The Malcolm Baldrige National Quality Consortium, formed by the American Society for Quality Control and the American Productivity Center, administers the evaluation process.

The Board of Examiners is composed of quality experts, including retired quality professionals, selected from industry, professional, and trade organizations and universities. Those selected meet the highest standards of qualification and peer recognition. Examiners take part in a preparation program based on the criteria, scoring system, and examination process.

In recognizing the first winners of the National Quality Award, President Reagan remarked that they "Exemplify the belief that quality counts, first, foremost, and always...they realize that quality improvement is a never-ending process, a company-wide effort in which every worker plays a critical part."

Many companies that have submitted applications for this highly coveted award have literally invested hundreds of thousands of dollars in time and effort in their quest to win. If successful, such an investment can pay off handsomely in terms of publicity and the enhancement of the corporate image. Winners of the award have included:

Company	Category	Year
Cadillac Motors	Manufacturing	1990
IBM	Manufacturing	1990
Federal Express	Service	1990
Wallace Company Inc.	Small Business	1990
Milliken & Company	Manufacturing	1989
Xerox Corp. Business Products/Systems	Manufacturing	1989

Motorola Inc.	Manufacturing	1988
Commercial Nuclear Fuel Division	Manufacturing	1988
Westinghouse Electric Corp.	Manufacturing	1988
Globe Metallurgical Inc.	Small Business	1988

Quality and service awards such as the Malcolm Baldrige National Quality Award are one of the best forms of packaging and selling to be found. A company that works hard enough to earn an award deserves to enjoy the ensuing benefits to its reputation and should do everything possible to promote its success.

Action Plan

1. Make a decision as to whether or not your company can better package and sell its commitment to quality and service.

2. Take your time and determine that you have a solid track record to stand on in terms of your customer sensitivity.

3. Prepare consumer education materials that will convey a "We Care About The Customer" attitude to the public. Avoid crossing the line and having such materials become too obvious of a commercial for your company.

4. Consider whether or not your organization can benefit from a warranty or money-back guarantee program. Be ready to stand behind your promises in a hassle-free manner.

5. Form a quality institute to serve as a means for conducting surveys, disseminating public awareness materials, sponsoring essay contests, establishing scholarship funds, and creating intern programs.

6. Remember to use the media to your full advantage to publicize newsworthy quality and service efforts undertaken by your firm and/or quality institute.

7. Incorporate a variety of direct marketing methods to inform the buying public of your abilities and dedication to delivering perfect products or services. Use slogans and mottos, buttons, media advertising, and quality newsletters as well as other creative techniques.

8. Seek quality awards whenever possible, including the Malcolm Baldrige National Quality Award. If you win, create a marketing campaign to let the public know.

9. Maintain your credibility through consistency in producing quality results. Challenge employees to always meet and exceed your company's standards for quality and service.

CHAPTER 8

Remember The
Customer In A Crisis

T he real test of an organization's customer sensitivity comes not with its normal day-in and day-out operations, but during a crisis. Undoubtedly everyone has experienced the crunch times when things seem to be unraveling. Do you remember that the customer is still king even during adversity, or do you head for the hills when the going gets tough?

There are many examples of how large, high-profile firms have missed golden opportunities to cement relationships with existing customers and win new customers, because of their handling of crisis situations. In 1989, the Exxon tanker *Valdez* ran aground in the Prince William Sound of Alaska, creating a spill of 11 million gallons of crude oil—one of the worst spills in history. In the following days, Exxon was lambasted by the press, conservation groups, and public officials. Naturally a disaster of this sort is bound to generate substantial negative publicity; however, a company can take steps to dilute such ill will. Many critics believe that Exxon did not act quickly or decisively to avert the public's negative perception that ensued.

Braniff Airlines is another example of how the customer was not the priority during a crisis. Braniff, which had been through bankruptcy in the early 1980s, was attempting to build a national airline from its hub in Kansas City. On September 25, 1989, during a speech to a Kansas City civic group, Braniff's president told of the airline's plans to significantly increase service to the local airport on the following Sunday, October 1. On Wednesday, September 27, Braniff abruptly stopped flying, and the following day it filed for Chapter 11 reorganization. Travelers were given no advance warning of the shutdown and thousands were stranded at ticket counters. It is hard to believe that Braniff did not know in advance that its financial condition was so precarious that bankruptcy was imminent. If it truly planned to reorganize and continue flying, why did it not wind up its affairs in a more orderly fashion, without destroying the goodwill of its customers?

In 1989 my wife and I took a winter vacation cruise on a ship with stops scheduled on a number of islands. As the week progressed, the ship stayed close to its primary port, making short day sails to neighboring islands. We were told that weather conditions prevented us from making the regular stops—though sister vessels were doing so at the same time. No one could figure out why the cruise was not going as planned or why the cruise line was stonewalling us. At the end of the trip, we learned from passengers of the sister ships that their captains had told them that our ship had an engine that was not operating thus the reason for staying close to the primary port. What's worse, we learned that the engine was down prior to our departure and apparently the cruise line had decided not to tell the passengers the truth about the problem. Not only were we upset, but many other passengers were furious, spending their time on the plane flight home discussing their displeasure. When I wrote to the company to express my feelings about this matter, I received no reply. I telephoned the president who did not return my call. After I wrote a second time, I finally got a response that was dated more than a month earlier, but was curiously postmarked just a few days before it was received. The explanation was shallow and did not begin to address my concerns. As a goodwill gesture, the company offered us a small discount on our next cruise. Will we ever vacation on this line again? No way!

These are all examples of companies under siege and how *not* to win customers. Psychologists talk about the human instincts of fight or flight. I believe there is a parallel in this philosophy where Corporate America is concerned. In a crisis, corporate management can stand and fight or it can avoid the issue by trying to protect its backside (hence, flight). Fighting does not necessarily need to be construed in the negative sense, but rather as a firm's commitment to stand up and take its lumps and make things right. Too often managers are more worried about their own job security than their customer satisfaction.

Plan Ahead

To properly manage a crisis, a company must first plan for it. Assemble staff members at all levels for a series of brainstorming sessions where every conceivable crisis is addressed. A department store, for example, should involve the store manager, department managers, sales associates, buyers, stockroom personnel, cashiers, and legal counsel. The store manager should invite everyone to help make a list of anything and everything that can go wrong in the store. Examples include:

- A major sale is advertised for a particular item and the store doesn't have it in stock.
- Price tags are mistakenly attached to the wrong items.
- Quality problems are found with an entire shipment of products.
- The sprinkler system activates and floods the store and its customers.
- Half the sales staff is stricken with the flu and cannot work during the busy Christmas season.
- A group of animal rights activists set up pickets to protest the store's sale of furs.
- The store is plagued by a series of purse snatchings.

One or more brainstorming sessions will probably result in a much longer list than the examples mentioned here.

This kind of exercise is healthy for department stores, restaurants, auto repair shops, supermarkets, health spas, bookstores—any and every business imaginable. The key is to get the participation and perspective of personnel involved with every aspect of the company. Consideration should be given to splitting up the brainstorming into two functions: (1) the creation of the list of crises and (2) the development of an action plan for each.

As solutions are discussed for meeting each challenge, the brainstormers must always keep customers as the central focal point. In each instance the solution that is formulated must start with the question, "How will our actions affect customers?" Unfortunately in today's litigious society, there is a very legitimate concern that the manner in which a company responds to a crisis could expose it to a lawsuit. If the department store gives a gift certificate to a distraught customer whose purse has been snatched, is it making some admission that its security is lax? If the store finds that it has advertised a huge sale on an item that it embarrassingly finds it doesn't have in stock, what is its exposure? Legal counsel should be a part of the brainstorming sessions to help the group navigate the murky waters of liability. Yet, the lawyers shouldn't be problem solvers where customer relations are concerned. Instead, participants must figure out creative ways to walk the tightrope between customer sensitivity and customer lawsuits, using the expertise of attorneys in the process.

Something to keep in mind as a crisis plan is developed is not just basic customer service, but how to make lemonade out of lemons. By putting the warm blanket around customers in negative circumstances, not only can the problem be neutralized, but it may also be turned into a plus for the company. The crisis-management group should look for ways to turn the potential wrath of customers into praise that will be carried by word of mouth to other potential customers. Suppose that at a fine restaurant the power goes out in the middle of the evening. After determining that the power cannot be restored in the next few hours, the diners finally gather their things and leave. How can this possibly be turned into a positive experience?

The savvy restauranteur and staff who have planned for such a remote disaster may graciously decline to charge any customers who have not finished their meal. And the restaurant owner might invite all patrons to return at another time for a free dinner, giving them makeshift certificates as they depart. Some might say that this is a terribly expensive gesture costing hundreds—maybe even thousands—of dollars. Will the customers come back? There is little doubt that most will, and they will probably tell their friends how incredibly well they were treated. Instead of losing customers, the restaurant conceivably could gain new customers as a result of its reputation for going far beyond what normally would be expected. The cost of the free dinners could be viewed as an investment in customer development.

More Training

After brainstorming crisis situations and how they will be addressed, the next step is to create a crisis plan book. This manual should be prepared by someone participating in the brainstorming sessions or, if the company is large enough to have a consumer relations department, its director is a logical choice. Each crisis should be carefully catalogued and the plan of action clearly detailed. The crisis plan book should not be a document that sits on a shelf and gathers dust. It should be constantly reviewed and updated. Figure 8.1 shows a page from the Cohen-Esrey Real Estate Services Crisis Plan.

All personnel should be given a copy of the crisis plan book and its subsequent updates. Crisis training is critically important at this stage. A formal training program revolving around the crisis plan book should be implemented for all personnel. This training format should be separate from a company's regular training effort to make an even greater impact with the firm's personnel. All new employees should be indoctrinated as to how business will be conducted in a crisis. Continuing crisis education for existing employees is a must, including the CEO and executive-level management. Role playing is one very effective training method—

FIGURE 8.1: Crisis Plan Book

COHEN–ESREY REAL ESTATE SERVICES INC.
Crisis Plan

Scenario: Sewer Backup On Lower Level Of Building

At 11:00 P.M., the sewer drains back up in an apartment building flooding all six occupied apartments on the lower level.

Step 1: The On-Site Manager must immediately contact the Maintenance Technicians and Custodian to meet him/her at the building.

Step 2: All staff members should arrive at the building within 10 minutes.

Step 3: The On-Site Manager should knock on each door and alert the residents that the property staff is there to address the problem.

Step 4: The Maintenance Technicians should begin checking to see where the blockage is in the sewer lines. If possible, eliminate the blockage. Once the scope of the situation has been determined, the On-Site Manager shall call the Property Manager if deemed necessary, who will come to the property if the problem is severe enough. If this is not warranted, the On-Site Manager shall notify the Property Manager the next morning.

Step 5: If the blockage cannot be removed using on-site equipment, the designated sewer cleaning contractor should be called immediately by the On-Site Manager.

Step 6: The staff should assist the residents in moving furniture and other personal property away from the flooded floor areas and wipe off any items that have been affected.

Step 7: The staff should immediately begin wet vacuuming the carpets to remove the sewer water. If necessary, pull back the carpets when completed and bring in fans to help dry the carpet. If the padding has been badly damaged, pull it up and dispose of it. Use a deodorizer on the carpet and pad if necessary.

Step 8: Before any member of the staff departs, the blockage must be removed, all sewer water vacuumed, and carpets pulled back and drying.

Step 9: The On-Site Manager shall inform each resident as to exactly what will be done the next day to complete repairs. If a resident is not home at the time the back-up occurs, a detailed note must be left explaining what has transpired and the planned action for the next day.

Step 10: The next day (even if it is a Saturday or Sunday), the property staff shall return to each apartment at the time indicated to the residents by the On-Site Manager the night before and make final repairs. Any further clean-up will be completed; new padding installed if necessary; the carpet resecured to the tack strip; and the carpet cleaned and deodorized. The staff will assist the resident in moving furniture and other personal property back to its original position, when the carpet is dry.

Step 11: The On-Site Manager will personally follow up with a visit to each resident and make certain that all clean up and repairs have been made satisfactorily. Any further resident requests will be so noted and addressed immediately.

Step12: If necessary, the On-Site Manager will offer to aid the residents in completing Renter's Insurance claim forms if any of their property was seriously damaged.

Step 13: The On-Site Manager will deliver during the visit to each resident, a small gift to each resident (a tin of cinnamon rolls, fruit basket, etc.) with a note apologizing for the inconvenience.

Step 14: With the Property Manager, the On-Site Manager will convene a short meeting of the staff after the crisis has passed to review the manner in which the team handled the problem. Corrective measures will be taken for any flaws that are discovered.

Step 15: Without fail the crisis will be resolved from start to finish within 24 hours.

similar to the fire drills that we all remember from our school days. During regular staff meetings at various levels, consider a pop quiz from time to time, on a specific crisis scenario. See how well the group is able to discuss the response that would be expected if such a crisis were to occur. If the staff is fuzzy or uncertain as to the proper course of action, schedule additional training.

Spring Into Action

The worst thing that can happen when a serious challenge appears is what I call the Crisis Freeze. The symptoms include a denial that a problem exists, stonewalling, fingerpointing, and similar behavior. A paralysis sets in and nothing is done to overcome the situation—in effect, the organization is frozen in its tracks. This is detrimental to customers in the short run, but the company is the big loser over the long haul as customers take their business elsewhere.

To avoid Crisis Freeze a company must spring into action immediately. If there has been an ongoing focus on dealing with crisis situations, if a crisis plan book exists, and if crisis training has been established, a firm will have little difficulty quickly taking steps to preserve customers' best interests when storm clouds gather. Consider creating a crisis team if the situation warrants, to coordinate a rapid, customer-sensitive resolution. This team could consist of management and employees from many different departments, especially those directly affected. It is important, however, that there be a team leader, most likely the CEO or some other executive-level manager.

Delta Air Lines utilized the team approach a few years ago when it was faced with a major crisis. In October 1987, the Department of Transportation published the first series of on-time airline figures, and Delta was near the bottom of the list. According to Hollis L. Harris, former president and chief operating officer, within hours of the announcement, a task force was in place and personnel at all levels of responsibility in each area went into an intense problem-solving mode. Harris stated:

> Falling short on on-time performance was a paradox of sorts for the Delta people. For 14^1/$_2$ consecutive years, the Delta Team had had the fewest number of service complaints per 100,000 customers boarded of all the major carriers. And, we have had the best mechanical dispatch reliability and the best flight completion record in the U.S. industry. But the task force paid little attention to those records. Rather, they subjected virtually every aspect of the operation to microscopic scrutiny, making major changes and minute tweeks that might improve our on-time record. When the D.O.T. figures for April 1988, were announced, the efforts of the Delta people paid off. It took Delta six months to go from near the bottom to the top of the list.

In a crisis, it is important for a company not to overreact. The problem needs to be analyzed instantaneously even if management and employees have to get out of bed or return from vacation. At the same time, the problem shouldn't be studied to death. The analytical phase is crucial to the implementation of the crisis plan, for if the components of the problem are erroneously identified, the real issues may not be properly resolved to customers' satisfaction. The crisis team that is assembled should be made up of individuals who have demonstrated analytical capabilities and have the experience and intuition to sort out the facts and keep their cool under pressure.

Communicate With Everyone

There have been previous references in this chapter to denials, stonewalling, and similar actions. All point to a lack of basic communication. When a crisis occurs it is more important than at any other time to adequately communicate with all parties. People generally want to know what is going on, even when everything is seemingly copasetic. But when things go haywire, the need and desire to know increase exponentially. By nature, humans fear the unknown, and in times of adversity the unknown creates high stress levels. A thorough understanding of this emotional response will enable an organization to develop effective communications that will defuse the potential volatility of a crisis.

Part of the crisis plan must include specific elements of communications—who, what, and when. Depending on the situation, it usually makes sense to designate a company spokesperson—possibly the CEO or an executive-level manager. Some companies make the mistake of allowing too many employees to be involved in the communication process, resulting in chaos and the dissemination of conflicting information.

To determine what needs to be communicated when, the company must put itself in the shoes of its customers. What will they want to know? In the example given in Figure 8.1 in which the apartment sewers were backed up and flooding, the first thing customers would want to know is, "Who is going to stop the flood and how quickly will they get here?" This will be followed by questions such as, "Who is going to clean up the mess, when is it going to happen, and what will happen to my furniture and personal belongings?"

If a company truly understands customers' needs, simple common sense will dictate how to anticipate what people will want to know and how to formulate a response. If possible, the company spokesperson should "be there in the flesh," to meet directly with the customers who are affected by the crisis. If this is not logistically feasible, then other media must be utilized, such as letters, media statements, telephone calls, telegrams, and paid advertisements in newspapers and on radio and television stations. It is imperative that communications be forthcoming as quickly as possible. Customers should not have to languish in a vacuum—the perfect environment for unfounded (and unflattering) rumors.

An ideal approach is for the company spokesperson to provide initial communications in a clear, no-nonsense manner with the appropriate amount of sympathy for customers. During this communication, the spokesperson may be able to outline the company's step-by-step plan to deal with the crisis. Above all, the spokesperson should explain precisely how the inconvenience or other negative impact will be resolved to customers' satisfaction. Thereafter, regular and frequent communications must be provided to update customers and make them aware of how the resolution is progressing. Such communications must continue until the crisis has passed.

In the summer of 1987, Delta Air Lines encountered a number of nationally publicized incidents, including a flight during which the cockpit crew inadvertently shut down both engines nearly causing a disaster. The senior vice president of marketing sent the letter shown in Figure 8.2 to Delta frequent flyers. Additionally the chairman and CEO sent a memorandum to each employee, explaining in detail the company's concerns, corrective actions, and pledge to quality service. (Figure 8.3.) This communication helped to overcome the negative customer and employee perception over Delta's safety lapses. It is an excellent example of how a company stepped forward and took responsibility for its actions—and communicated with its customers in the process.

A company's communications process must involve customers and employees. For all employees to function as a team to meet a crisis, they too must be kept informed at all times. A company handicaps itself when its personnel is in the dark as to what the crisis plan entails. Employee morale will plummet especially in crises that receive a great deal of media coverage. Employees who must answer the questions of their friends about the situation will be less likely to do so in a positive fashion if they are uninformed. This fosters further suspicion and ill will on the part of the public.

Employees must be told in meetings and through written communications about the crisis. The communique should identify the problem, why it happened, and the step-by-step plan to correct it. Additionally, employees should be told exactly how they will be a part of the solution.

FIGURE 8.2: Delta Air Lines letter to its frequent flyers.

August 14, 1987

Dear Frequent Flyer:

You have selected Delta for a substantial amount of your travels and we sincerely appreciate it. By your making this selection, we have always thought of you as part of the Delta family—a matter we take very seriously.

We also take very seriously our responsibility to provide you with the finest and safest air transportation in the world. In keeping with this responsibility, we feel an obligation to share with you the attached memo written to all Delta personnel by Ron Allen on July 31, 1987, regarding the incidents involving Delta between June 18 and July 12 which received so much media attention. (At the time the memo was written, Ron was our President and Chief Operating Officer. He has since become our Chairman and Chief Executive Officer.)

Your overwhelming support during this very trying period has been extremely gratifying to all of us here at Delta. The cards, letters, phone calls and comments many of you have made to the media have sustained us through these very difficult times. It is during times like these that people's true colors are shown and when real friends become highly visible.

We are proud to have you as friends and customers, and we renew our pledge to you to provide you the finest airline service possible. All of the slashing comments, jokes, political cartoons and questionable reporting cannot erase the fact that Delta has the finest service record of any airline in the world. We owe it to you to keep it that way, and we will.

Thank you for being so special.

Sincerely,

W. Whitley Hawkins
Senior Vice President—Marketing

FIGURE 8.3: Delta Air Lines memorandum to its employees.

July 31, 1987

Message to the Delta Family From Ron Allen, Chairman of the Board and Chief Executive Officer:

The events which have occurred over the past month have been puzzling and frustrating for you just as they have been of deep concern for all of us in the management of Delta. From June 18 through July 12, we had a series of five isolated but significant incidents. That is unusual in any airline but, to say the least, in Delta.

Rather than take the time in this memo to outline again the events of each one of those incidents which have been so well publicized, I simply wanted to let you know that each individual incident has been carefully investigated. While each had several contributing factors, human error or a breakdown in cockpit discipline appears to be the primary cause. As such, positive corrective action and firm individual disciplinary action have been taken where appropriate. While these individual incidents have been disappointing, I feel without a doubt that we have the finest and most professional pilot group in the industry and they have my complete support, admiration and trust. No one has felt any worse about the recent events than the members of our pilot staff.

As a result of this aberration in the operation of our company, the media (newspapers, radio and television) has singled us out to monitor almost every flight in our system, and we have such things as flat tires and loose monkeys in the cargo bin appear as front page or prime time news. In addition, we have become the focal point of many jokes. I know this hurts you as it hurts me. The safety and professionalism of our operation is something we take very seriously and never joke about.

How do we as individual members of the Delta family respond to this negative reflection on our company? How do we answer questions from the customers whom we are privileged to serve? How do we react to the media, our neighbors, our friends, etc., who wonder if something has changed at Delta? There is only one way we can respond—to be clear that Delta has not changed, that the best, safest, most caring service possible remains our overriding objective, and that the incidents they have witnessed are truly an aberration in no way indicative of Delta Air Lines' operation.

We must respond with the same professional attitude toward service to our customers and dedication to our individual responsibilities that we have shown over our many years.

Each of you is well-qualified and has been well-trained for the position that you occupy. I ask you to re-dedicate yourself to doing your individual jobs to the absolute best of your ability, whether it be flight attendant, pilot, agent, mechanic, or other position in the field or in the general office. If at any time you have questions about the best way to perform your part of our operation, it is important that you seek answers so that the traveling public whom we are privileged to serve continues to see Delta as the airline run by professionals and as the world's premier air transport company.

When you are asked by others about Delta and what we stand for, you can remind them that over many years Delta has earned an outstanding reputation for the best in air transportation that we are still the first choice of most pilot applicants as they apply for positions in the airline industry, that Delta has more cities staffed with maintenance personnel than any other airline, thereby ensuring that our professionally-trained mechanics maintain our airplanes in the safest possible manner, and that Delta has had the fewest number of passenger complaints of any airline since 1974, a record in which you can take much pride. You can remind them also that Delta still has one of the best overall safety records in the industry.

It is important not to overreact and respond in a negative way to the overreporting and unusual scrutiny of the press. The media has a job to do, and it is news when an airline such as Delta has such an unusual series of events. It is important that we speak with one voice. This is why you have seen most of the interviews with Delta conducted by Bill Berry, our Director of Public Relations. As you can well imagine, Bill and his staff in public relations have been under a tremendous amount of pressure having calls coming to their offices and homes 24 hours a day. We have been very open and responsive to the media inquiries and have tried to react in a direct and factual way to every question, while at the same time pointing out the positive aspects and the contributing factors of each situation. On the other hand, we do hope that we are near the end of the media's overzealous publication of events that occur in our day-to-day operation (which normally would never even be mentioned) while events on other airlines of a much more serious nature have occurred and either go unreported or are buried somewhere deep in the midst of other news.

Recently, there have once again been several favorable news articles about Delta. Much of this is the result of interviews with individual members of our Delta family. We welcome the media to come in and look at our operation. We only want them to provide objective and complete coverage without singling us out and trying to make news out of something which is not.

Thank you for your patience, your dedication and your understanding as we go though this difficult time. Remember that a true test of the strength and character of people is not measured so much during the good times when things are going well and everyone is saying nice things about you, but instead in those difficult times such as we have experienced in the past 30 days. These are the times in which we must redouble our efforts to pull together as a team to demonstrate to all concerned that Delta truly is a caring and highly-professional family made up of individuals who are dedicated to serving the traveling and shipping public.

Dealing With The Media

Many crises occur without ever attracting a great deal of public attention. An incident of significance, however, can generate the kind of media interest that often isn't favorable. Media encounters can be used to neutralize negative circumstances and in some cases create a positive image for the public. Using media communications to the benefit of customer relations requires careful thought and planning. The international public relations firm of Fleishman-Hillard, Inc., suggests the use of the following media interview guide when preparing for a media encounter.

MEDIA INTERVIEW GUIDE

If a reporter calls, determine why he is calling and the subject to be discussed. Ask if he is on deadline; assure him you will call back before deadline.

Quickly Prepare:

- Jot down likely questions, appropriate answers.
- Know what you want to communicate. Plan to make your points accordingly.
- Have public relations staff research, prepare information, provide background.
- Call the reporter back.

The Interview:

- A broadcast interviewer may want a "voice level." This sets his recorder sound.
- Resist the urge to half-shout into the telephone or microphone. Ask if you are being heard.
- Offer your conclusion first, briefly and directly. Back it with facts.
- Avoid company jargon, acronyms.

- Be realistic, positive.
- Never lie to a reporter.
- Short answers are better than long; use full sentences.
- Be honest, responsive, factual. Don't talk too much.
- Don't accept a reporter's facts and figures as true; don't respond to a hypothetical situation; respond to negative leading questions with positive statements.
- Keep cool. Don't allow yourself to be provoked.
- Remember when talking to a reporter there's no such thing as "off the record."
- If there are any skeletons in the company's closet, be prepared for them to come up in the interview.
- State matter of factly when you can release information and why.
- If you don't know answers, say so, and offer to find out.
- Use the reporter's name.
- Don't overlap the interviewer's question; begin your answer when he is finished.
- Learn how to deal with unfavorable situations. Be forthright yet be prepared to not necessarily answer questions.
- If the interview is negative in tone (or is being conducted by an investigative reporter), you may want to tape-record the interview.

The interview will be brief. A reporter has only a few minutes to get your full story. Don't ask to approve the story before it is published or broadcast.

Suggestions For A Television Interview:

- Dark clothes, a blue shirt look best on television.
- Be sure the background is an appropriate setting for the interview.
- Take 45 seconds to straighten your hair, tie, shirt.
- If you wear photo-gray glasses, take them off for the interview.

- Stand up straight; look directly at the reporter, not at the camera or the microphone.
- Smile only at appropriate times.
- Resist the urge to shout into the microphone.
- Relax. Be factual.
- The session will be brief. You have only about 30 seconds to make your point on videotape.
- If you are set up—if a reporter asks for an interview to discuss one subject and begins asking questions about another subject, wait until the question is asked and say, "I thought this interview was to be about _____ ." You may tell him that you are not in a position to discuss the other subject.
- Following a two or three question interview, the cameraman will want to shoot additional videotape. The microphone will be off. The reporter will then ask you to chat about the weather, Sunday's football game, etc. Be sure your movements (smiles and gestures) are in accordance with your posture during the interview.

Copyright by Fleishman–Hillard, Inc.

Turn It Around

A crisis can be a nightmare for a company—many have bumbled and stumbled to the point that one almost feels sorry for those perpetrating ineptitude. Conversely, challenging situations can be golden opportunities to make lemonade from lemons. Sharp, customer-sensitive managers will be constantly on the lookout for ways to make this happen should they find themselves in a crisis. Attitude has a lot to do with whether or not this can be accomplished. The crisis team that is negative and defeated from the start will probably be negative and defeated at the finish line. On the other hand, if the team can maintain a positive outlook and truly attempt to resolve the problem in the customer's best interest, the chances are good that positive results will be attained. The attitude of the team is a direct reflection of the attitude of the team leader; therefore, it only makes sense to have this individual have a dynamic, positive, and enthusiastic personality.

An example of converting a negative situation into a corporate victory occurred in the summer of 1985 when Coca-Cola made the ill-fated announcement that it was changing its soft drink formula. After introducing the new product, the company received as many as 12,000 phone calls a day and 68,000 customers wrote letters, mostly in protest of the change. Coca-Cola's CEO, Roberto C. Goizueta, recalled two of his favorite letters.

Dear Sirs:

I am disgusted, disenfranchised, dismayed, disillusioned, disputatious, dispirited, disdainful, disheartened, displeased, disserviced, discordant, disputant, and disprised with feelings of disloyalty.

P.S. I love Diet Coke.

Gentlemen:

I would appreciate receiving your signatures on a piece of Company stationery. I believe that in years to come, the autographs of two of the dumbest executives in business history will be very valuable.

Material used with permission of The Coca-Cola Company.

A consumer rebellion was in full swing and threatened to be one of the most embarrassing crises ever faced by a U.S. corporation. Coca-Cola expanded its toll-free 800 telephone operation to handle the crush of calls and even retained the services of a psychologist to help study the public's reaction. He and his associates listened to, and in some cases even fielded, consumer calls. The psychologist reported that by allowing customers the opportunity to vent their frustration over the loss of their "old friend," Coca-Cola was able to maintain brand loyalty that could have been lost.

Coca-Cola listened to customers, compiled statistics on a daily basis, and reviewed consumer sentiment with top-level management. Market research surveys were also conducted, and it was obvious that the company's miscue had become a full-blown crisis. Shortly thereafter, the firm reintroduced the old formula as Coca-Cola Classic and reported that it received 18,000 telephone calls expressing thanks for the move. According to Coca-Cola, product sales skyrocketed. The company received enormous publicity, and by staying in touch with customers' needs and reacting quickly, Coca-Cola restored its image and possibly gained from the experience.

Johnson & Johnson, and its affiliate McNeil Consumer Products Company, were stung twice by tampering with its Tylenol medicine. Fatal cyanide poisonings involving Tylenol capsules occurred in Chicago during 1982 and in New York during 1986. In response to the 1982 incidents, Johnson & Johnson took the following steps:

- Tylenol capsules were removed from the market.

- They were reintroduced 60 days later in a triple-seal, tamper-resistant package, making Johnson & Johnson the first in the industry to respond to the national mandate for tamper-resistant packaging.

- To encourage consumers to purchase the product, the company provided free coupons worth $2.50.

- Salespeople worked to recover former stock and shelf facing levels by implementing an off-invoice pricing program and providing buyers with discounts linked to wholesale purchasing patterns—discounts as high as 25%.

- A massive new Tylenol advertising program was launched.

- More than 2,250 salespeople were asked by Johnson & Johnson to make presentations to physicians and others in the medical community in support of the capsule reintroduction.

- A toll-free consumer hot line was established during the first week of the crisis, with more than 30,000 calls handled during the first 60 days.

- A full-page ad was placed in major newspapers across the country offering consumers the opportunity to exchange capsules for tablets.

- On two separate occasions, Johnson & Johnson wrote letters to its domestic employees and retirees, keeping them updated on the situation.

- A 60-second spot was broadcast featuring the firm's medical director, alerting consumers to the impending return of the Tylenol capsules in tamper-resistant packaging.

- Members of the Corporate Relations Department visited more than 160 congressional offices in Washington, D.C., to lobby for legislation making product tampering a felony.

- Johnson & Johnson executives made personal appearances or were interviewed by many television, radio, and newspaper media.

- All letters from consumers to the company were answered directly by Johnson & Johnson's Corporate Public Relations Department.

In 1986, with the Westchester County, New York, poisoning, Johnson & Johnson repeated many of the same efforts that were utilized during 1982, including recalling all Tylenol capsules nationwide. Press conferences were held and an 800-number telephone hot line was established. The company then announced its decision to permanently discontinue the manufacture, distribution, and sale of capsule products made directly available to consumers. Capsules were replaced with caplets that are much less susceptible to tampering.

As a result of its prompt and forthright handling of the Tylenol incidents, Johnson & Johnson was able to manage the damage and enhance its corporate image. Today, Tylenol continues to be a dominant product in over-the-counter analgesic medications, and Johnson & Johnson is viewed by consumers as a good and caring public citizen. This is truly another excellent example of how a company turned around a potentially devastating crisis to its benefit.

Action Plan

1. Don't let a crisis erode your customer base by bumbling and stumbling.

2. Plan for crises by holding a brainstorming session during which every conceivable crisis is identified. Include management and employees at all levels of the company.

3. Develop a crisis plan that addresses each potential challenge and create a crisis plan book to be distributed to all employees.

4. Train employees to understand their role in a crisis and how the company will react when a crisis arises.

5. Spring into action. Don't succumb to the Crisis Freeze. Avoid stonewalling, fingerpointing, and similar behavior. Instead, form a crisis team to analyze the problem and implement the crisis plan.

6. Don't overreact to a crisis—get the facts and analyze them properly. At the same time, don't study the problem to death.

7. Designate a company spokesperson. Interact directly with the affected customers in person or by written correspondence, telephone calls, media statements, and advertisements —whatever works best.

8. Communicate with customers immediately. Outline a step-by-step plan to resolve the situation in the best interest of the customer. Maintain regular and frequent communications during the crisis to update the progress of the plan.

9. Don't forget to communicate with company employees from the outset. They need the same information as customers as well as how they play a role in resolving the crisis.

10. Be prepared when dealing with the media. Never lie to reporters. Try to neutralize the negative aspects of the situation if at all possible.

11. Try to turn lemons into lemonade. Look for an opportunity to turn the crisis into a benefit for customers and the company. Always maintain a positive and enthusiastic attitude.

CHAPTER 9

Can It Be Done Profitably?

N ow the question focuses on the bottom line. Can creative customer service be performed profitably? The answer is obvious that it can. But just how profitable is a bit more challenging. Certainly a company has to do more than just be dedicated to its customers to stay in the black. I know of a small travel agency that epitomizes customer service, yet it is losing money. Why? For one reason: The owner doesn't track accounts receivable adequately. There is no billing system for hotel and car rental commissions, and if a payment is not received, little is done to pursue it. Profitability is a blend of many elements, including understanding the customers' needs, providing quality products or services designed to meet those needs, and following up to see that customers are satisfied. Furthermore, tight controls must be in place to keep production and distribution costs as low as possible, debt must be maintained at reasonable levels, accounts receivable should be vigorously pursued, and sales methods must match or be better than those of the competition. An imbalance in any of these factors can be enough to start the flow of red ink. Witness the recent spate of mergers and leveraged buyouts. Solid companies, many with strong commitments to customer satisfaction, have fallen on hard times as a result of shouldering mountains of debt resulting from their acquisition or restructuring.

Quality + Service = Profits

Thus, the relationship between profitability and customer service is difficult to quantify. It is safe to assume that excellent quality service will generate repeat business, which in turn can boost sales. Higher sales can mean more profits if the products or services are properly priced so that there is still something left after all the bills are paid.

As I wrote this book, I became more curious about the profitability of the various companies I was researching. Most of the large companies are listed on public stock exchanges and publish financial data regularly. The corporate entities that I selected to study are generally regarded as having strong customer awareness by various standards of measurement. This includes everything from media articles to publications by the American Management Association and other industry groups. A review of customer service practices of such firms generally supports the perception that they are, in fact, leaders. Finally, personal experience with a number of these companies further validates this perception.

How profitable are the large corporations surveyed for this book? With help from the Value Line service and *Forbes* magazine, statistical data were compiled comparing the various companies with their industries in terms of return on equity and sales growth. *Forbes* magazine (January 7, 1991) published its "Annual Report On American Industry" which calculated 5-year return on equity and growth rates—through April–December 1989 for firms with fiscal years ending in those months, and through January–March 1990, for firms with fiscal years ending in those months (see Figure 9.1). Return on equity was computed by taking primary earnings per share and dividing it by common shareholders equity per share at the beginning of the year. Gains or losses from discontinued operations were included, but not extraordinary items. *Forbes* figured sales growth rates using the least squares method.

For purposes of evaluating customer service the preceding comparison is not scientific and this author does not purport that

FIGURE 9.1: *Forbes'* "Annual Report on American Industry"

Company	5 Year Return On Equity (%)	Industry Median (%)	5 Year Sales Growth (%)	Industry Median (%)
Albertson's	22.7	16.0	9.6	11.0
Amdahl Computers	18.9	13.8	24.3	12.6
American Express	21.4	20.1	19.5	16.7
BankAmerica	3.1	1.3	(6.0)	7.9
Campbell Soup	10.4	20.0	8.4	10.5
Chrysler Motors	18.6	18.6	12.5	10.5
Citicorp	7.1	1.3	13.1	7.9
Coca–Cola	39.1	22.8	11.0	11.0
Delta Airlines	16.9	8.2	13.9	18.1
Dillard's	18.2	15.2	18.5	6.5
Disney	26.4	14.3	21.6	18.0
Federal Express	10.3	10.3	27.6	15.9
General Cinema	46.6	14.3	19.9	18.0
General Electric	19.0	17.2	12.7	10.1
Giant Foods	24.8	16.0	9.0	11.0
Goodyear	17.7	14.9	2.1	8.7
H. J. Heinz	25.8	20.0	8.2	10.5
Hilton Hotels	16.1	20.9	8.8	8.8
J. P. Morgan	1.9	1.3	8.5	7.9
Johnson/Johnson	26.5	19.1	10.4	10.4
Kellogg's	39.0	20.0	12.8	10.5
K–Mart	13.2	13.3	6.9	14.8
Liz Claiborne	40.2	22.5	29.1	12.2
Marriott	24.5	15.7	17.6	15.9
Maytag	26.9	12.7	9.8	13.9
McDonald's	22.2	14.9	13.1	12.4
Merck Drugs	44.6	20.6	14.7	11.9
Motorola	12.3	13.8	12.6	12.6
NIKE	26.8	22.5	10.9	12.2
Nieman–Marcus	N/A	15.2	13.9	6.5
Nordstrom's	20.2	20.2	21.8	14.6
Ralston–Purina	43.5	20.0	4.4	10.5
Rubbermaid	22.9	15.6	19.7	15.0
Spiegel	24.2	15.0	18.1	19.4
United Airlines	30.8	8.2	7.8	18.1
Wal–Mart	36.0	13.3	32.5	14.8
Westinghouse	23.6	17.2	21.3	10.1
W.W. Grainger	17.6	17.2	10.8	10.1
Xerox	10.1	16.3	9.7	11.7

N/A = Not Available

Note: 5–year return on equity and sales growth are average annual figures.

there is any clear statistical correlation. It is extremely interesting, however, and, I believe, more than coincidental that 33 of the 39 companies equaled or exceeded their industry's 5-year median return on equity. Only 25 of the 33 companies equaled or exceeded their industry's 5-year median sales growth; this statistic does not have the same relationship as return on equity. As companies become larger, it becomes increasingly difficult to sustain high annual sales growth figures. At the same time, profitability can still be maintained at high levels even though sales don't continue increasing exponentially. This is why it is truly amazing that a giant such as Wal-Mart has been able to sustain a 5-year average annual return on equity of 36% and 5-year average annual sales growth of 32.5%!

With a new emphasis on customer service, W. W. Grainger, the heating, air conditioning, electrical, and plumbing equipment and parts distributor, saw its sales increase by 16% in 1988 and earnings increase 20%. Nordstrom department stores, widely renowned for its service philosophy, saw its sales increase from just over $900 million in 1985 to nearly $2.9 billion in 1990, and net income increased during the same period from $40 million to $101 million. Additionally, Nordstrom's $380 in sales per square foot was nearly double the industry average for 1988. The Walt Disney Company has seen revenues increase from $1.45 billion in 1984 to $5.84 billion in 1990, and net income increased from $97.8 million to $824 million—a growth of 742% in the bottom line over five years!

The success stories are so numerous that they could fill another book. The point is that companies that utilize good business practices find that having a "Customer Is King" attitude *is* good business.

Cost Efficiencies

Another way to look at profitability was explored in Chapter 5, "Do It Right the First Time!" When 20% to 25% of the cost of gross sales relates to product deficiencies in America's manufacturing sector, it's easy to see how the profit picture could be vastly improved for many companies with a focus on better quality. As a company begins to accomplish this, new ideas will be generated, not only to eliminate defects in products or services, but also to be more efficient in all areas of operation.

Purchasing agents will start looking for ways to negotiate with suppliers to shave a few percentage points from the cost of materials. Data processing teams may figure out ways to save on the use of computer paper. Plant managers could figure out how to implement new preventive maintenance systems that will reduce the cost of equipment repairs. The shipping department might develop a delivery program that will be more cost-effective in getting products into customers' hands. These efforts do not need to be viewed as belt tightening, as much as they are the brainchild of creativity and improvements to internal quality and efficiency.

To stimulate participation in instituting cost-efficiency measures, a number of companies offer bounties to employees or employee teams whose ideas result in such savings. A percentage of the savings (within preestablished parameters) is paid in cash to the responsible employees. This approach recognizes the fact that enhancing profitability stretches from the top to the bottom of an organization.

Recession Proof?

In the Gallup Organization's survey for the American Society for Quality Control, the question was asked, "Is a company any less susceptible to the effects of recession, compared to other companies in its industry, if it is the quality leader in its industry?" Of the executives polled, 73% believed that quality-leading firms are less likely to feel the effects of a recession: 83% answered affirmatively for large companies; 63% for small companies; 68% for service companies; and 80% for industrial companies. This response further supports the theory that quality and service go hand-in-hand with profitability.

Profit is not a dirty word nor should profits be viewed by the public with "robber baron" connotations—provided that such profits have been obtained honestly and ethically. Profit is merely a by-product of outstanding quality and superb customer service. If the products or services they are acquiring have such traits, consumers will generally regard corporate profits in a benign manner. Only when the public hears of companies with huge earnings, but knows that they have taken advantage of others or provided substandard quality or service, will it react with disapproval.

CHAPTER 10

The Final Ingredient

This book has been an attempt to explore a relatively complex subject in common sense terms. But there's a final ingredient that we've barely touched on that is the key to making quality and customer service an absolute success. This ingredient is like yeast is to bread—without it, the bread won't rise. This ingredient is the yeast for a solid quality service program—without it, everything discussed in this book is reduced to academic theory.

The final ingredient is...**PASSION**. *Webster's* defines passion as "enthusiasm, zeal; intense emotion compelling action." Passion also happens to be the most elusive, the most intangible factor that the people in an organization can possess. Let's further define passion as it relates to quality and service.

Passion is...

- Employees putting customers' needs before their own. An analogy to this is, "Don't close the restaurant if there's still one more customer who wants to eat." How many times have you seen this happen—literally? The poor guy races to the door of the restaurant at 10:01 P.M. just as the hostess locks the door. She shakes her head and points to the sign indicating that closing time is at 10:00 P.M.

- Handling rude and outraged customers with diplomacy, grace, *and* a smile. No doubt you've witnessed just the opposite where the salesperson tells the customer that she can take her business elsewhere and then seeks coworkers' approval by rehashing the incident for the next 30 minutes.

- Doing something the right way even though no one else is watching. It is so easy to cut corners and do so in a way where the chances are great that no one will ever know.

- Accepting full responsibility when things go wrong. The urge to point fingers can be mighty strong when the fire starts getting hot.

- Going above and beyond the call of duty to help customers. How about the salesclerk who finds a customer's wallet and, after calling the person's home for hours only to get no answer, delivers it personally to the customer's home?

Passion is doing what you enjoy so much that at the end of the day you don't want to stop. Not for the money (overtime pay or extra sales), but for the pure love of what you are doing. Then when you finally shut off the lights and go home, there's an incredible sense of self-satisfaction in knowing that you've done your very best.

Passionate people should not be confused with workaholics. Workaholics are driven by obsession and may be trying to escape from their problems by throwing themselves into their work. People with passion may work a lot as well, but they do so because, as *Webster's* put it, "intense emotion compels action."

So how can a company instill passion in its employees? Passion can't be *taught*; however, passion can be *caught*. It is a contagious quality that will spread like wildfire. Passion is like riding a bicycle. With nourishing, the innate sense of balance eventually manifests and is never forgotten. Passion too is innate and with encouragement can manifest and come to fruition. It's not a matter of whether one person has it and another does not. It's simply a question of what the trigger factor will be.

Triggering passion starts at the top of the organization. Chairmen, presidents, or CEOs must have complete, unwavering passion for quality and service if they expect everyone else to do the same. Just as the corporate goal must be 100% perfection in the production of goods and services, the CEO's goal should be 100% passion among the troops. If employees see their leaders passionately living, eating, breathing, and sleeping quality and service, this may be the example they need to trigger their own sense of passion.

CEOs should continually ask employees, "Are you happy? Are you having fun?" Corporate management should strive to enable employees to answer these questions affirmatively. If this all sounds too warm and fuzzy, stop and think for a minute. Are you more productive when you're happy and having fun, or when you're unhappy or apathetic?

Maintaining employee satisfaction doesn't necessarily mean opening the checkbook, though employees need to be fairly compensated and genuinely encouraged. A more critical aspect is the environment of the work place. Is teamwork encouraged? Is safety paramount? Does laughter exist? Do people clearly know what is expected of them and how to do their jobs? Company policies must be flexible enough to allow employees to express their passion and to do whatever it takes to satisfy customers.

Passion is an eternal crusade to think of new ways to make customers happy—not because it's just good business or makes the cash register ring a few more times, but because you truly like to make people happy. In one of the office buildings we manage, we implemented a policy of doing all sorts of little unexpected things for our tenants. At Christmas we delivered poinsettia plants. Every so often we will bring a box of doughnuts to each office, and recently we put jars full of candy on the desk of each receptionist throughout the buildings. The cost of these items was miniscule and the customer reaction was gratifying. The tenants couldn't believe that we cared enough to make such gestures. One of the senior partners in a major law firm that decided to leave the building told me that had we been managing the building before his firm made the decision, they might be staying instead. The greatest part about all of this is that the concept of passion has been caught by the building staff. They are now, unprompted, starting to look for ways that they can do things to make the building tenants happy.

Knowing the fundamentals of quality and customer service isn't enough. Living and practicing them so as to recognize each customer as a human being is part of the process. Then you must do whatever it takes to personalize service in such a way that it makes each individual customer ecstatic. Now that's real passion! You can't know passion. Passion is not a state of mind, but a state of the heart. When Corporate America finally realizes this, watch out Japan!

CHAPTER 11

And Everyone Lived Happily Ever After

S o there you have it; the story about customer service. The story of how the frog prince (played by the customer) is kissed by the princess (played by the company) and is ultimately crowned as king of the land. Is it a fairy tale or is it reality?

Quality and customer service are still myths to some businesses, but during the 1990s many of these firms will either learn this script or become extinct. Foreign competition will be stiffer than ever. The Japanese show no sign of weakening and the European Community, post-1992, will be a formidable trading force. Many companies are already starting to awaken to the notion that quality and service are critically important to quarterly earnings.

The Gallup Organization's survey for the American Society for Quality Control asked the question of 601 executives from the 1,000 largest companies listed by *Fortune* magazine, "What are the two most important things your company is doing to improve customer satisfaction with your company's product or service?" The answers, shown in Figure 11–1 were quite diverse. The same survey also inquired, "In the next three years, how critical will the following issues be to your company? (Rated on a 10-point scale with '10' meaning the issue is extremely critical and '1' meaning not at all critical.)" The results are shown in Figure 11.2.

The company with its ideals grounded in quality and service will understand that it all begins at the top of the organization. Managers at all levels will constantly rub shoulders with their

FIGURE 11.1: What companies are doing to improve customer satisfaction.

	Total %	Large Companies %	Small Companies %	Service Companies %	Industry Companies %
Better customer relations/follow-up	38	38	37	37	39
Improve quality of service	28	24	33	31	23
Provide top quality products	20	20	20	16	26
Employee education /training	19	18	20	25	7
Install quality control program	12	13	11	8	19
On-time delivery	8	8	8	6	11
Employee motivation	6	6	7	8	4
Low cost	5	3	6	5	4
Develop in-house programs	5	7	4	6	5
Upgrade inspection of products	5	4	6	4	7
Closer monitoring	3	3	2	3	1
Market research	3	4	2	3	3
Good knowledge of inventory	2	2	3	3	2
Telephone services	2	2	3	3	2
Miscellaneous	2	1	4	4	1
Nothing	1	1	*	*	2
Don't Know	2	3	*	1	3
Number of Interviews	601	298	303	381	218

*Less than one-half of one percent.

customers to find out what they really think. Managers will be good listeners during customer interactions. Creative ideas will abound and customer service will become the centerpiece of every staff meeting with an eye on how customers will be impacted by corporate decision making. Employees will be hired who are intuitively service minded, with quality and customer service viewed as important corporate assets. Everyday little actions will reflect a customer-first attitude.

FIGURE 11.2: Future Critical Issues

	1986 %	1987 %	1989 %	Change 87–89 %	Large Companies %	Small Companies %
Service quality*	41	48	54	+6	51	58
Product quality*	41	39	51	+12	51	51
Productivity	31	26	32	+6	30	34
Government regulation	20	19	25	+6	22	28
Product liability	17	14	18	+4	10	24
Cost of materials and labor	16	14	22	+8	15	27
Capital available	14	14	15	+1	12	18
Labor relations	12	14	14	0	11	16
Rapid response in bringing products and services to market	N/A	N/A	26	N/A	26	25
Number of Interviews	698	615	601		298	303

N/A = Not Available

* In the 1986 survey, product and service quality were one category. In the 1987 and 1989 surveys, product and service quality are two separate categories.

More emphasis will be placed on getting to know customers. Daily personal one-on-one encounters will evolve to generate customer feedback on what they will pay, what level of quality they desire, how quickly they need the products or services, and what the competitive alternatives are. Demographics and other factual data will be used with regularity to better understand customers' needs.

First-rate organizations will develop overall customer service strategies utilizing a task force of employees from all areas of the company. Credos may be established as a pledge to consumers. Technological advances will be incorporated into daily operations, including computerization and communications to better serve customers. Corporate managers will remember that technology broadens the customer base; but at the point of sale, the encounter must be personalized.

Training is going to take a front seat with the focus on getting the job done right the first time. Employees can look forward to written job descriptions that help them understand the performance standards expected, but with enough flexibility to allow them to meet customers' needs. Corporate universities or cooperative programs with local colleges may become common, utilizing video and audio productions and classroom and seminar forums. Written manuals are destined to become streamlined and continuing education will be a requirement for everyone. Finally, customers can count on salespeople having a complete understanding of each product they sell.

In the 1990s, inferior or defective products and services may become things of the past with companies striving for 100% perfection. Employee recognition programs for superior quality will go hand-in-hand with teamwork, company spirit, and reduced employee turnover. To avoid complacency, job functions may be rotated when possible, with improvements realized in the work environment. American consumers can bet that more capital resources will be made available to keep plants and equipment in state-of-the-art form. Vendors should be ready for greater scrutiny of the materials they supply.

As the decade advances more customer follow-up can be expected with CEOs and upper-level management taking active roles. Methods to be utilized include point of purchase surveys, questionnaires, follow-up phone calls, and customer encounter groups. More companies will "shop" their salespeople to determine marketing prowess. Management teams will carefully review customer reactions and follow up further to ensure 100% total customer satisfaction. Lots of "lemonade" will be made with complaints and suggestions viewed as opportunities to further cement customer relationships.

As businesses become more adept with service, and quality reaches new heights, we can expect to see more packaging and selling of the "We Care About The Customer" attitude. Warranties and money-back guarantees will prevail. Consumer education materials should find their way into the marketplace with increasing frequency, and the public may see more corporate commitments made to establish quality institutes. Young people may be more indoctrinated with principles of service and quality as a result of more publicity on the subject. We'll probably see more slogans, mottos, buttons, media advertising, and quality newsletters touting companies' customer awareness. The Malcolm Baldrige National Quality Award may become one of the most coveted prizes in American history.

When future crises do occur, enlightened management will have a plan in place to deal with the situation. Training will emphasize how to react to a crisis, with a crisis plan book as standard reading material. The Crisis Freeze will thaw with well-trained company spokespersons soothing consumers through honest, straightforward communications that also meet the employees' need to know.

Not every company will enjoy record profits. Some companies will still do better than others—after all, that's the price of free enterprise. But with improvement in quality and service consciousness comes the opportunity to regain market share lost to foreign competition. Companies with this awareness should be better able to weather downturns in the economy as they occur.

Clearly, passionate employees will create companies characterized by zeal and enthusiasm. The passion revolution will sweep the country with superb quality and unequaled service. Passion at the top can trigger passion throughout the organization with employees living, eating, breathing, and sleeping service and quality.

Truly, the American people will be the beneficiaries and American companies will be richer when...The Customer Is King!

Index